THE SECOND WORLD WAR
SECOND EDITION

D0185364

CONTENTS

1 APPEASEMENT: 1938–9

Key Issues

- Why did Chamberlain support appeasement?
- Did appeasement make war more likely?

Appeasement is the term used to describe the foreign policies of the Conservative governments of Stanley Baldwin (1935–7) and Neville Chamberlain (1937–40). Appeasement involved making concessions to Hitler, the **dictator** of Germany, to peacefully settle German complaints about the terms of the Treaty of Versailles. The hope was that by making concessions to them, another terrible war, like the First World War, could be avoided.

March 1936: German troops marched into Rhineland, breaking the Treaty of Versailles

March 1938: Austria united with Germany, breaking the Treaty of Versailles

Oct. 1938: Germany allowed to occupy the Sudetenland

March 1939: Germany seized the rest of Czechoslovakia

August 1939: Germany and the Soviet Union secretly agreed to invade Poland together

Sept. 1939 Germany invaded Poland

How Germany expanded its borders, 1936–9.

THE TREATY OF VERSAILLES

The treaty which ended the First World War, the Treaty of Versailles of 1919, left Germany a bitter nation. Politicians at the time believed that as long as Germany felt this way there would never be lasting peace in Europe. Chamberlain agreed with this opinion and he took a favourable view of Hitler's complaints about how unfair the treaty had been to Germany. He believed that if Germany's complaints were dealt with fairly then Europe could look forward to a long period of peace.

This wasn't Chamberlain's only reason for supporting appeasement. Britain was still suffering from the effects of the **Great Depression** and Chamberlain was reluctant to spend vast sums of money on improving the country's armed forces. Weak defences, he believed, wouldn't matter if Britain avoided war. Britain was more worried about defending its empire in Asia and had been concerned about the threat from Japan in the Far East. It couldn't deal with aggression from both Germany and Japan. Besides, public opinion supported appeasement and Chamberlain, therefore, was only doing what the people wanted.

THE MUNICH AGREEMENT

Hitler gradually ripped up the terms of the Treaty of Versailles and there was only the mildest of protest from Britain. However, the Sudetenland was a different issue from Rhineland and Austria (see map above) because it belonged to Czechoslovakia, which had no intention of giving it up to Hitler. Hitler demanded that it become part of Germany because three million Germans lived there.

Chamberlain, Daladier for France, Hitler, and Mussolini, the **fascist** dictator of Italy, all met in Munich in September 1938 and decided that the Sudetenland should be handed over to Nazi Germany. This was known as the Munich Agreement. The Czechs were not consulted and were given no choice but to agree.

Churchill bitterly attacked the Munich Agreement in the House of Commons (see Source A). If Germany did go to war with Britain or France later, then they would regret the loss of 'the fine Czech army'. The Czech army was well equipped and numbered about 500,000 men – not much smaller than Germany's. Six months later, in March 1939, Hitler ordered German troops to seize the rest of Czechoslovakia. He broke every promise made at Munich.

At last, Chamberlain and Daladier realised that they could not trust Hitler to keep his promises. They both offered Poland an alliance. If Germany invaded Poland, where about one million Germans lived, Britain and France promised to defend the Poles. Hitler took little notice of this alliance. Why should he? Britain and France had done nothing over the Rhineland, the takeover of Austria, the Sudetenland, or even Czechoslovakia. Why should things be any different over Poland?

THE NAZI-SOVIET PACT

The only country Hitler was worried about was the Soviet Union (Russia). He was afraid that a German invasion of Poland might lead to war with the Soviet Union. He *did* want a war with the world's only **communist** power – but not yet. In late August 1939 the Nazis and the Soviets met and agreed a pact. This was called a non-aggression pact because they promised not to go to war with each other. But secretly they also agreed to invade and divide Poland between them. Germany would invade on 1 September and Russia later in the month.

A SOURCE

Speech by Winston Churchill in Parliament on the Munich Agreement, October, 1938 (adapted from *Britain and Europe*, ed. J Joll, 1967).

I will begin by saying what everybody would like to ignore or forget but which must nevertheless be stated. We have experienced a total defeat. The government has neither prevented Germany from re-arming, nor did it re-arm ourselves in time. Thus, they have left us without adequate national defence. If the Nazi dictator should decide to attack us in the west, then France and England will bitterly regret the loss of the fine army of Czechoslovakia . . . and do not suppose that this is the end. This is only the beginning.

B SOURCE

Chamberlain's policy at Munich (from *Britain in Modern Europe*, E Nash and A Newth, 1967).

Chamberlain gave Hitler everything he wanted. Hundreds of thousands of Czech citizens and the magnificent defences of their frontier were handed over. It was not only Czechoslovakia that was ruined. We and the French had lost a good cause and our good name. We had lost a well-armed ally on Germany's southern frontier. We re-armed during this year [1938–9], but not to equal the Czech arms which had been thrown away. Chamberlain did not realise the disaster he had helped to create.

C SOURCE

A definition of appeasement (adapted from *British History*, eds J Gardiner and N Wenborn, 1995).

Linked with the policies of Stanley Baldwin and Neville Chamberlain, appeasement was later condemned as a cowardly policy of sacrificing smaller and weaker countries in an unsuccessful bid to prevent war. Combined with the failure to re-arm, it led to the criticism of pre-war leaders for bringing Britain to the brink of defeat in 1940.

D SOURCE

The British newspaper, the *Guardian*, reports on Chamberlain's return from Munich, October 1, 1938.

He drove from Heston airport to Buckingham Palace, where the crowd called for him, and within five minutes of his arrival he was standing on the balcony of the Palace with the King and Queen and Mrs Chamberlain. The cries were all for 'Neville' and he stood there waving his hand and smiling. For three minutes this demonstration lasted.

E SOURCE

Aircraft built by Britain, France and Germany, each year from 1936 to 1939 (from *The Rise and Fall of Great Powers*, P Kennedy, 1988).

	1936	1937	1938	1939
France	890	743	1382	3163
Britain	1877	2153	2827	7940
Germany	5112	5606	5235	8295

F SOURCE

Crowds outside Number 10 Downing Street, cheering Chamberlain after his return from Munich.

Questions

a What can you learn from Source A about Churchill's views on the Munich Agreement?

b Does Source C support the evidence of Sources A and B about the Munich Agreement?

c How useful are Sources D and E as evidence of the success of appeasement?

d 'Chamberlain's policy of appeasement was the right policy at the time.' Use the sources and your own knowledge to explain whether you agree with this view.

2 AN OVERVIEW OF THE WAR

Key Issue

- What events marked turning points after the war?

The Second World War in Europe can be roughly divided into two periods. The years between 1939 and early 1942 were mostly years of victory for the **Axis** powers of Germany, Italy and Japan. Towards the end of 1942 the war began to turn against the Axis. From then on, the years between late 1942 and 1945 were ones of triumph for the **Allied** powers of the USA, the Soviet Union and Britain.

This chapter is a brief outline of the main events of these years.

YEARS OF AXIS VICTORY

Germany's new form of warfare, ***Blitzkrieg***, or lightning war, brought a string of rapid victories. German troops invaded Poland in September 1939 and overran the Polish forces within a month. This was a task made easier by the invasion of eastern Poland by the Soviet Union (Russia) in the same month. The Russians occupied eastern Poland while the Germans took the western half. This had been agreed in the Nazi–Soviet Pact in August (see Chapter 1).

The Germans occupied Norway in April 1940. This ensured that vital iron ore supplies would continue to reach German factories. It was now that Hitler decided on his boldest move: the invasion of France in May 1940. The conquest of France in June represented the greatest success of Hitler's *Blitzkrieg* strategy (see Chapter 3).

British forces were driven out of France after their evacuation from the beaches of Dunkirk in June 1940, leaving much valuable equipment behind. But 330,000 British and French troops had escaped (see Chapter 5). Britain waited for the expected German invasion. The German air force tried to destroy Britain's Royal Air Force during the Battle of Britain in August and September 1940, but failed (see Chapter 6).

RAF cadets training in 1942. At first glance it would seem that these cadets would have to pedal very hard to get airborne, and that their chances against a German fighter were not very encouraging. In fact, they're practising formation flying.

INVASION OF RUSSIA

Hitler decided to put aside his plans for the invasion of Britain. His attention was really elsewhere since his main ambition was to conquer Soviet Russia. In June 1941 the decisive event of the war in Europe took place as three million German troops invaded Russia. By 15 October the Germans were only 100 kilometres from Moscow (see Chapter 8).

After helping to defeat Poland, the Russians attacked Finland in November 1939. The Finnish–Soviet War (November 1939–March 1940) was not part of the Second World War but it was a very costly victory for the much bigger Soviet forces against the well-equipped Finnish troops (above). The Russian army did so badly that Hitler was convinced – mistakenly – that a German invasion of Russia would be easy.

WORLD AT WAR

The war became a true world war in December 1941 when Japan launched a surprise attack on the American fleet in its Pacific base at Pearl Harbor and followed this with attacks on British bases in the Far East (see Chapter 13). Germany and Italy, in support of their Axis partner Japan, declared war on the USA as well. The Japanese captured the British naval base at Singapore in February 1942. They took prisoner 62,000 British, Australian and Indian troops.

Italy's declaration of war on Britain and France meant that the war included North Africa. Here, British forces scored some early successes against the Italians. German troops were sent to the assistance of their Axis partner in February 1941. The German–Italian army drove the British back from their earlier conquests.

YEARS OF ALLIED TRIUMPH

The Axis run of victories came to an end at the battle of El Alamein in November 1942. Italy itself was invaded in July 1943 and surrendered in September to the Anglo-American forces.

In the same month as El Alamein, the Germans were facing an even more devastating defeat in Russia at Stalingrad. At first, the victories had come easily as the Russian Red Army broke and retreated. At Stalingrad, though, the Russians held their position and turned the tide against Hitler, eventually defeating the Germans in January 1943. The Germans tried one final offensive at the battle of Kursk in July 1943. It failed and from then on the Germans were constantly on the retreat (see Chapter 9).

Germany's failure against Russia convinced the British and Americans that the time was right to strike a blow against German-occupied Europe in the west. In June 1944 Allied forces landed on the beaches of Normandy in France. The surprised Germans were unable to drive the Allies back into the sea, and in August Paris was freed from Nazi rule.

The Allies made slow progress from the west while the Russians advanced from the east. There was a setback for the British at Arnhem in September 1944. The Germans made one final – and unsuccessful – effort to prevent an invasion of Germany itself. In December they launched the Ardennes Offensive (or 'the Battle of the Bulge'). Early in 1945 Allied troops moved into German territory and the Russians occupied Berlin in April. Hitler shot himself at the end of that month and on 8 May 1945 Germany surrendered. The war in Europe was over.

MIDWAY

Retreat became a new experience for the Japanese as well. After Pearl Harbor Japanese naval and land forces had swept aside all opposition in the Pacific. But the naval battle of Midway in June 1942 put a stop to these victories as the Americans sank four Japanese aircraft carriers. 1944 saw two further decisive American victories at sea over the Japanese: the battles of the Philippine Sea (June) and Leyte Gulf (October).

In April 1945 the Americans took Okinawa and from there they could launch an invasion of Japan itself. In August the USA decided to make use of their new, secret weapon. Two atomic bombs were dropped: one each on the cities of Hiroshima and Nagasaki. A week later on 15 August the Emperor of Japan, Hirohito, agreed to surrender. The formal surrender was signed in September 1945. The Second World War was over.

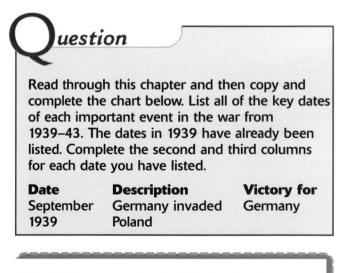

Question

Read through this chapter and then copy and complete the chart below. List all of the key dates of each important event in the war from 1939–43. The dates in 1939 have already been listed. Complete the second and third columns for each date you have listed.

Date	Description	Victory for
September 1939	Germany invaded Poland	Germany

Make brief notes under the following headings:
- Blitzkrieg
- Invasion of Russia
- Stalingrad
- Pearl Harbor
- Normandy landings
- Japan's surrender

3 BLITZKRIEG

→ **Key Issue**

• Why was *Blitzkrieg* so effective?

Hitler had prepared for a short but vigorous war. Germany had a small number of well-trained and equipped mechanised units, that is tanks, supported by motorised infantry (troops in trucks). It was vital for Hitler that the war he planned was both short and limited. This was because Germany didn't have enough supplies or weapons to fight a long war on more than one front.

Artillery and dive bombers began the process by 'softening up' the enemy. They shelled the enemy front and rear, increasing panic and fear. The panic created among the civilian population had two purposes. It damaged morale and also drove thousands of frightened civilians onto the roads. These civilians jammed the roads as they fled away from the fighting. At the same time, the troops of the country being attacked were trying to use the same roads to bring up reserves. Confusion took over.

SURPRISE IS THE KEY

Surprise was a key factor in the German success. The attacks on Poland and Soviet Russia were surprise ones. Most of the Polish air force, like the Russian one later in 1941, was so unprepared that it was destroyed on the ground. The French had less excuse because they had been at war with Germany for nine months when they were attacked. What surprised them, though, was the direction of the attack (see

A SOURCE

General K Nehring, a German officer who took part in the invasion of France, writing in 1979 (from *Blitzkrieg*, L Deighton, 1979).

In 1940 the French Army was still considered the most powerful in the world. Allied forces were stronger in terms of tanks and superior in numbers to the Germans. What the Allies lacked were new ideas. Despite what they had seen happen in the Polish campaign, the Allies still relied on the Maginot Line for protection and thought only about defence and a slow, long campaign.

Chapter 4). Once again, Hitler had seized the decisive initiative.

Germany's *Blitzkrieg* strategy concentrated armoured columns of tanks and troops in lorries at the key, weak points of the enemy defences. They used their concentrated fire-power, speed, and greater numbers at these points to smash their way through the enemy's positions. They went round the better-defended positions and cut them off from reinforcements. The infantry on foot could deal with these later. While this was happening, paratroops (soldiers dropped from planes) were busy seizing enemy HQs, telephone exchanges, or bridges. Then they would wait for their own fast-moving armoured columns to catch up with them.

SUCCESSFUL TACTICS

Clearly surprise, speed and concentrated fire-power were very important, but these cannot explain everything. The Poles, the French, the British, and later the Russians, all confronted the Germans with out-dated tactics. They had failed to understand the vital role that the tank would play in the war. The

B SOURCE

A map showing the German attack on France and the Maginot Line.

tank should be an independent weapon and not tied down by having to protect slow-moving infantry.

German equipment was not really any better than that of the **Allies**. The British and French had more tanks than the Germans in 1940. Indeed, the best tank of the war at this stage was French, and the best tank of the whole war was the Russian T34. Germany's armed forces weren't any bigger but they were put to better use. Both the British and French used their tanks in small numbers, spread thinly among their troops. The Germans grouped their tanks in highly effective armoured units. In this way, the German tanks were always able to outnumber those of their enemy because the Germans chose where they would fight their battles.

But the Germans did have a crucial advantage in aircraft numbers over the French and Poles. This was important in helping them achieve their stunning victory in 1940.

C SOURCE

A modern history book (from *Finest Hour*, T Clayton and P Craig, 1999).

The supposedly unbeatable Maginot Line in which France had put her trust, stretched from Switzerland to the Ardennes forest. But northward from there, along the border with Belgium, the Maginot Line was only pillboxes and barbed wire put in place the previous winter. It was through these weak defences that the German tanks had smashed.

D SOURCE

French troops are shown here digging trenches somewhere behind the Maginot Line in 1940.

E SOURCE

Military forces of France, Britain and Germany involved in the German invasion of France, May 1940 (from *The Oxford Companion to the Second World War*, ed. I C B Dear, 1999).

	Aircraft	Tanks
France	1368	3063
Britain	456	310
Germany	4020	2445

F SOURCE

A modern history book on how the French used their tanks in 1940 (from *The Oxford Companion to the Second World War*, ed. I C B Bear, 1995).

The French Army was powerful on paper; it had more tanks than the Germans, and some were better, but it had not yet grasped the idea of grouping them together in large numbers. This was how the Germans had already triumphed in the Polish campaign. Part of the French tank strength was instead spread out thinly and ineffectively – ready, like a lot of small corks to plug holes in the line.

Questions

a **What can you learn from Source A about Allied military thinking in 1940?**

b **Does Source C support the evidence of Sources A and B about the German invasion of France in 1940?**

c **How useful are Sources D and E as evidence about why France was defeated in 1940?**

d **'Germany's success in 1940 was due to better weapons and better tactics.' Use the sources and your own knowledge to explain whether you agree with this view.**

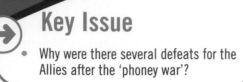

Key Issue

- Why were there several defeats for the Allies after the 'phoney war'?

THE DEFEAT OF POLAND

The Germans occupied Poland without too much difficulty by the end of September, after launching their surprise invasion on 1 September 1939. Poland's problems were made that much worse when the Russians invaded from the east on 17 September. This had been agreed between Russia and Germany in their non-aggression pact in August (see Chapter 1).

Britain and France both had a treaty with Poland and declared war on Germany on 3 September 1939. But this made little difference to Poland. The British and French chose not to do the one thing they could have done to save Poland. This was to invade Germany while the bulk of the German armed forces were involved in Poland. The British and French (not to mention the Poles) were to pay a heavy price for this reluctance to begin the war seriously.

THE PHONEY WAR

For the British and French, the first seven months of the war were rather dull – there was no fighting on land between them and the Germans. This period (September 1939–April 1940) was called, at the time, the 'phoney war' (because there wasn't much fighting during these months). Instead of making jokes about the 'Bore War' or 'Sitzkrieg', the British and French should have been learning the lessons of *Blitzkrieg*. The phoney war came to a dramatic end in April 1940 when Germany invaded and occupied Norway. The British and French troops sent to oppose the Germans achieved little.

The loss of Norway was a setback which led to a new government in Britain. Chamberlain, Britain's Prime Minister since 1937, was widely seen as the man who had failed to stop Hitler, and Parliament decided a more aggressive leader was needed. That man was Winston Churchill – though it's worth remembering that Churchill was a member of Chamberlain's government at the time. He had long

been a critic of Chamberlain's **appeasement** policy before the war and didn't think much of Chamberlain's half-hearted efforts against Germany during it. He became Prime Minister of a **coalition government** of Conservatives, Labour and Liberals on 10 May. From now on, the British government would fight the war with a real sense of purpose and determination.

THE INVASION OF FRANCE

The loss of Norway was a setback to the **Allies**, but worse was to follow in May. On 10 May Germany invaded Belgium, Holland and then France. Once again, the Germans caught their enemies unprepared. The overwhelming defeat of France in just six weeks was Hitler's greatest military campaign of the war. He planned and carried it out against the advice of his more cautious generals. But, as on other occasions, the victory was mostly due to the fine quality of his troops and the bungled plans and efforts of his enemies.

The French High Command was sure that their expensive line of underground forts, the Maginot Line, would protect France from a German attack. It probably would have done, if the Germans had decided to attack the Line – but they didn't. A key feature of *Blitzkrieg* was that the attackers avoided the enemy's strong points. The Maginot Line only protected France along its border with Germany. Hitler decided to attack at Sedan on France's border with Belgium.

The French had thought that the Ardennes Forest, to the north east of Sedan, was too dense for tanks to pass through. They were wrong. French resistance crumbled as the German tanks raced to the Channel coast in an effort to cut off the retreat of the 250,000 strong British Expeditionary Force. Guderian, the German tank commander, covered a remarkable 320 kilometres in ten days. But for once, caution got the better of Hitler and he ordered Guderian to halt his advance on Dunkirk. This was the port from which the BEF and some of the French army would try to escape to Britain.

A SOURCE

A modern history book on the early stages of the war (adapted from *A People's War*, Peter Lewis, 1986).

The RAF was mainly occupied in dropping leaflets, not bombs, on the Germans. When it was suggested in Parliament that a fire-bomb raid could set fire to the Black Forest in Germany, a government minister became angry: 'It is private property!'

B SOURCE

A modern history book on the early stages of the war (from *The Military History of World War II*, ed. Barrie Pitt, 1986).

In the meantime, 18 million printed leaflets informing the Germans of the wickedness of their Fuhrer, Hitler, would be dropped over Germany by the RAF. At the same time, they would ensure that no damage whatsoever occurred to German citizens' private property, in case it annoyed them.

C SOURCE

A modern history book on the early stages of the war (adapted from *World War 1939–45*, Peter Young, 1966).

The bombing of German cities might have relieved the pressure on Poland to some extent. But even Churchill took the view that American public opinion would be disturbed if Britain began to bomb German cities before the Germans had bombed Britain. The RAF had to settle for dropping millions of leaflets over enemy territory.

D SOURCE

'Very well, alone.' A British soldier is shown standing on Britain and facing towards Europe, after France's surrender; from the London *Evening Standard* newspaper, dated 18 June 1940.

E SOURCE

Part of a speech by Winston Churchill to Parliament, 4 June 1940.

We shall go on to the end. We shall fight in France, we shall fight on the seas and the oceans . . . we shall defend our island, whatever the cost may be. We shall fight on the beaches, we shall fight on the landing grounds, we shall fight in the fields and in the streets, we shall fight in the hills; we shall never surrender.

F SOURCE

A modern history book on British morale in the early stages of the war (from *The Ministry of Morale*, Ian McLaine, 1979).

There was certainly no evidence in the period between September 1939 and May 1940 pointing to the widespread existence of defeatism, but reports reaching the Ministry of Information spoke of . . . boredom and frustration. Morale appears to have been lower during this period than at any other time during the war. Having gone to war to defend Poland . . . the British government seemed to stand by while Poland was crushed by the Germans.

Questions

a What can you learn from Source A about the Chamberlain government's policy in the early stages of the war?

b Does Source C support the evidence of Sources A and B about the government's policy in the early stages of the war?

c How useful are Sources D and E as evidence of the state of public morale in the first eight months of the war?

d 'The first nine months of the war were a disaster for Britain.' Use the sources and your own knowledge to explain whether you agree with this view.

5 DUNKIRK AND THE BEF: 1940

Key Issue

- Dunkirk: miracle or disaster?

The British government had hoped that as many as 50,000 troops would be rescued from France in late May 1940. In the event, over 225,000 British and 110,000 French troops managed to escape from Dunkirk by ship between 26 May–3 June 1940. This happened mostly by night when the *Luftwaffe* could not operate. It was a remarkable achievement, right under the noses of the encircling Germans. The British press and radio hailed the evacuation – Operation Dynamo – as the 'miracle of Dunkirk'.

A number of factors contributed to this achievement. Most importantly, Hitler surprisingly ordered his tanks to halt outside Dunkirk and left the job of 'finishing off' the British Expeditionary Force to the *Luftwaffe*. However, RAF fighters fought off many of the German aircraft and the *Luftwaffe* failed. The British people responded enthusiastically to help with the evacuation. Most of the 850 ships involved were owned by civilians. They sailed across the Channel and ferried men from the beaches to the bigger Royal Navy vessels. Sometimes they even sailed all the way back to the English coast. 250 of these rescue ships were sunk. However, the British did have the satisfaction of knowing that their wrecks now clogged up the harbour at Dunkirk and made it useless to the Germans.

FRANCE BETRAYED?

Nonetheless, it was also a shattering defeat. Britain had clearly abandoned its only ally as well as huge amounts of vital equipment – 475 tanks and 1000 artillery guns were left behind. The French felt betrayed. In the early stages of the evacuation only one French soldier was being taken off the beaches of Dunkirk for every ten British soldiers. The French complained and Churchill issued orders that French troops should be treated the same as the British. The evacuation had only been possible because 30,000 French troops defended Dunkirk from the encircling Germans. The Germans later captured most of these. Churchill took a realistic view of Dunkirk. 'Wars are not won by evacuations,' he told the House of Commons.

The French felt even angrier when Churchill refused to send 120 Spitfires to France to help the French Air Force. As far as Churchill was concerned, these planes were now needed to defend Britain as France was clearly beaten.

France surrendered on 22 June and the Germans got hold of two years' worth of oil supplies. Hitler allowed a pro-German French government, led by Marshall Petain, to rule the south of France from the town of Vichy. This area became known as **Vichy France**. The north of France and its west coast were directly under the control of the Germans. A similar development took place in Norway where a Norwegian Nazi, **Quisling**, headed the pro-German government there.

A SOURCE

The Daily Mail's report of the evacuation of Dunkirk. This extract is from one reporter's interviews with the men evacuated back to England on 1 June 1940.

An artillery man told me that with thousands of others he had spent two days among the sand dunes with little food and no shelter from the German dive bombers.

Yet the men still joked, played cards and even started a football game to keep up their spirits . . . A sailor told me that a vessel in which he had been assisting on the Belgian coast had been sunk. No sooner had he and all his comrades landed [in England] than they all volunteered to go back at once.

B SOURCE

British troops returning by train after their evacuation from Dunkirk, 2 June 1940. The soldier is displaying a captured German rifle.

C SOURCE

Norman Wilkinson, an official war artist at the time, painted *Little Ships at Dunkirk*. A variety of vessels can be seen: a Royal Navy destroyer with a German bomb exploding nearby; Thames sailing barges; a large yacht still painted in peacetime white; coasters towing lifeboats packed with soldiers.

D SOURCE

The Evacuation from Dunkirk (from *Finest Hour*, T Clayton and P Craig, 1999).

Despite the loss of many valuable warships, the evacuation had been a fantastic success. Over a third of a million men had been brought out from directly under the guns of the enemy. Only about thirty thousand of the rearguard, almost entirely French, had been captured.

Questions

a What does Source A tell us about the evacuation from Dunkirk?

b Why were photographs like Source B officially approved at the time? Use Source B and your own knowledge to answer this question.

c How useful is Source C to an historian studying the evacuation from Dunkirk, 1940? Use Source C and your own knowledge to answer this question.

d Is Source D an accurate interpretation of the evacuation from Dunkirk? Use Source D and your own knowledge to answer this question.

6 THE BATTLE OF BRITAIN

Key Issue

● Why did Hitler fail to invade Britain?

CONTROLLING THE SKIES

After the fall of France, Britain expected a German invasion at any time. But before it could take place the Germans had to gain control of the skies. To do this they had to destroy the Royal Air Force (RAF). Once the RAF was defeated, the Germans would be able to bring their troops across the Channel without being attacked from the air. The Royal Navy, without the protection of the RAF, in the narrow waters of the Channel, would be an easy target for German aircraft. Everything, therefore, hinged on whether the *Luftwaffe*, the German air force, could eliminate the RAF. The Battle of Britain, from July–September 1940, was fought between the RAF and the *Luftwaffe* to see who would control the skies. This battle would decide whether an invasion would take place or not.

After France's defeat Hitler had offered peace terms to Britain. Some members of the British government, such as Lord Halifax and Neville Chamberlain, were keen to discuss these terms. They believed that Britain had little chance of resisting a German invasion. However, Churchill was not interested in negotiating with Hitler. Britain would fight on and his stubborn defiance helped to inspire the British through the next six, dark months. In the meantime, all that stood between Britain and a German invasion were 800 RAF fighter planes, under the command of Air Chief Marshall Dowding.

Fighter pilots 'scrambling' for their Spitfires. The Spitfire was the best fighter plane of the war in 1940, but Hurricanes played a bigger role in the RAF's victory. The pilots shown here are 'Free French' – those who chose to continue fighting alongside Britain under the command of de Gaulle rather than surrender to the Germans in June 1940.

German night-time bombing led to a black-out of city streets. The white line seen here on the pavement was to keep pedestrians from walking into each other by keeping on one side of the line. The black-out also applied to cars' headlights at first. But, after 1500 people had been killed in road accidents by December 1939, the government allowed cars to be driven with headlamp covers with small slits in them.

GOERING'S STRATEGY

Goering, the *Luftwaffe* commander, did not follow a consistent strategy. At first, the Germans bombed naval **convoys** and ports in the hope that the RAF would commit planes to defend them, but Dowding kept them back.

By the middle of August the Germans were convinced that the RAF had only 300 fighters left. In fact, the number was 600. Goering, therefore, concentrated on a target he knew that Dowding would have to defend: fighter airfields. By doing this, he was sure he could destroy the RAF's few remaining fighter planes. The German raids did not destroy many planes, but they did prove to be destructive, as the damage to runways meant planes couldn't take off from them.

Raids on aircraft factories would have been important in the *long-term*, but the RAF had no difficulty replacing aircraft – it was replacing pilots that was the crucial problem. Perhaps the most serious error made by Goering was his failure to attack the radar stations with any real force. Radar provided early warning of German raids and gave RAF Fighter Command time to get its aircraft up to their effective, operational height.

The RAF was finding it very difficult to make up its losses in pilots and the battle was going in Germany's favour – but the Germans didn't know it. The victory over the RAF which Goering had promised in August seemed no nearer in September. Hitler lost patience.

7 SEPTEMBER 1940

September 7 proved to be the turning point of the battle. Hitler, outraged by a British bombing raid on Berlin in late August, ordered a switch in tactics. He told Goering to bomb London and other major cities in an effort to terrorise Britain into surrender. The RAF was caught by surprise by this change of tactics and few RAF fighters opposed the attack. This, however, helped to convince Goering that the RAF was indeed on the point of defeat and so an even bigger raid was planned for September 15. For Dowding, the change of tactics brought welcome relief. The factories could turn out 500 fighters a week and the damaged airfields could now be repaired as the *Luftwaffe* concentrated on less vital targets like London.

The massive raid on 15 September saw 1000 German bombers and 700 fighter escorts attack London. But this time Dowding was ready for them. The RAF claimed to have shot down 185 German aircraft at the time. The actual figure was about 60 for the loss of about 30 RAF fighters. These exaggerated figures, though, were believed at the time and did a great deal to keep up civilian morale. During the entire Battle of Britain the RAF lost about 800 fighters while the *Luftwaffe*'s losses were about 1300 aircraft destroyed.

SEA LION POSTPONED

Though the bombing of Britain's cities, the Blitz, continued until May 1941, Hitler gave up on 'Operation Sea Lion' – the plan for the invasion of Britain. It was postponed on 17 September 1940 and quietly forgotten about. Hitler's real ambitions were to the east. His chief concern was to invade Russia. He decided to leave Britain alone for the time being since, in his view, Britain was no threat to Germany anyway.

The RAF was able to defeat the Germans mostly because of the foolish change in tactics on 7 September. The Spitfire – the best fighter plane at the time – also helped, as did radar. Radar gave advance warning of air attacks and allowed the enemy to be intercepted long before it reached its target. In this way, Dowding was able to concentrate his limited number of fighter planes at the right point at the right time. Furthermore, the *Luftwaffe*'s fighter aircraft had only about twenty minutes flying time over southern England before their fuel ran out, so they could only provide limited protection as escorts for their bombers. It's worth adding, also, that Hitler was probably never really that interested in invading Britain.

A SOURCE

A modern history book describing the situation at the RAF base at Manston in late August 1940 (from *Fighter*, L Deighton, 1979).

Many airmen had been sitting in air raid shelters ever since the last German attack at lunchtime on August 12th. Now the terrified men would not budge. While the RAF were in the shelters, local civilians took the opportunity to steal RAF tools and spares from the damaged buildings.

B SOURCE

The British weekly magazine, *The Spectator*, in an article dated 13 September 1940.

The immediate aim of the Blitzkrieg no doubt is to break morale. In that it will fail. The first attack was on our shipping. It was so totally unsuccessful that our convoys today go their way almost untouched. The second was on our airfields. It was applied with spectacular success in Poland. Against British airfields success was almost non-existent. Not a single one has been made unusable. The blows against our ports and dockyards have failed.

The Daily Mail's front page after the big German raid over London on 15 September 1940.

THE DAILY MAIL. Monday, September 16, 1940.

Daily Mail
FOR KING AND EMPIRE

LATE WAR NEWS SPECIAL

NO. 13,852 ★ ★ ★ MONDAY, SEPTEMBER 16, 1940 ONE PENNY

165 GREATEST DAY FOR RAF

(and more) DOWN

MORE than 165 German 'planes and at least 320 airmen were shot down in the morning and afternoon attacks on London yesterday.

The R.A.F. lost 30 machines and 20 airmen. In addition, German losses include: **18** on Saturday

Million Cheer London Battle

By Daily Mail Raid Reporters

HUNDREDS of German 'planes attempted to raid London, the Thames Estuary, and towns in the South-east yesterday—and they suffered their biggest defeat of the Blitzkrieg at the hands of our defences.

London had revelled in a 'quiet night.'

There was an alarm for only two hours in the middle of the night, but most people slept through it to the south...

'Massed' Fighters in Action

INVASION FLEET IS CRIPPLED

By NOEL MONKS, Daily Mail Air Correspondent

THE German Air Force returned to mass daylight raids on the Thames estuary and attempted to smash through to the London area yesterday, only to run into the greatest concentration of Spitfires and Hurricanes ever seen over this area.

The results were devastating, for German losses up to last evening were 165 'planes and at least 330 airmen.

On Saturday night the R.A.F. gave the invasion ports their most severe battering to date.

The ports of Antwerp, Ostend, Flushing, Dunkirk, Calais, and Boulogne were heavily bombed by strong forces.

Supply depots at Osnabruck, Mannheim, Aachen, Hamm, Krefeld, and Brussels were attacked, and also rail communications.

Pilots and crews pressed home attacks in spite of severe weather. Gun emplacements at Cap Gris Nez and enemy aerodromes were also bombed.

It is considered in R.A.F. circles that at least a quarter of Hitler's invasion fleet of barges and supply ships have been sunk or damaged as a result of our bombing attacks on the Channel ports.

This may not stop the invasion attempt, scheduled to start any day, but it must have caused serious disorganisation and confusion.

As an added hazard for London's night raiders, a new type of balloon barrage has been added to our...

Palace Bombed Again

RAIDER WRECKED

BUCKINGHAM PALACE was bombed again yesterday for the third time, when two heavy bombs and a number of incendiaries were dropped in a daylight attack.

The King and Queen were not in the palace. The heavy bombs which fell failed to explode—and the raider was shot to pieces by Spitfires a few seconds after the attack.

One of the crew baled out, but his parachute did not open, and he crashed on a roof.

GREEN to RED FOR 'GAS'

26 FT. DOWN

WEST DOOR

THIS *Daily Mail* picture-diagram shows the task that faced the St. Paul's bomb squad. You can see the direction in which the bomb was slipping, 26ft. down, threatening the Cathedral more and more each moment.

3-Day Battle with Time-Bomb

6 ENGINEERS HAVE SAVED ST. PAUL'S

By Daily Mail Reporter

A LITTLE party of Royal Engineers—an officer and five men—have saved St. Paul's Cathedral from terrible damage and possible destruction by a German time-bomb which fell from a 'plane on Thursday and buried itself 26ft. deep in a crater near the walls.

Yesterday at noon, after three days' continuous work, the bomb was secured by steel tackle and hauled to the surface with a pulley and cable attached to a lorry.

A City fireman who had been on duty continuously in the area told me:

"There were five of them, all young fellows, officered by a French-Canadian. One was an Irishman and a couple came from Yorkshire. Another, I believe, came from Lancashire.

"On the first day they couldn't start work, because a gas-main, broken by the bomb, was blazing. But they've been here from early morning till dusk ever since.

"It was wonderful to watch. They used no scaffolding or supports, and there was a risk of the road falling in at any moment.

"After digging through gravel and sand they came to black mud. The bomb was still slipping along through this almost horizontally, and in 24 hours it would have tunnelled under the Cathedral steps.

"But at last they got it. I heard one of them shout down the crater, 'Have you got it yet?'—and at last the answer, 'Yes. Here it is! Listen!'"

Leon Blum Arrested

VICHY, Sunday.—M. Leon Blum, the former French Premier and Socialist leader, has been arrested, it was announced here to-day. M. Blum was Premier in 1936 of the first Popular Front Government in France.

He is 67, a Jew, and an uncompromising opponent of Nazism.—B.U.P.

.". Captives May Not Meet !—Back Page.

Westminster Abbey Hit

The west window of Westminster Abbey was slightly damaged during a recent air-raid.

"The damage was very slight, and only a few small squares were broken," said an official.

LATEST 175 DOWN

In addition to 171 German 'planes shot down yesterday up to 10 p.m. by fighters, four cut straight across London at great height and top speed. They dropped several bombs in Central London.

BOMBS ON CENTRAL LONDON

Early raiders last night did not stop to encircle London. Defying the A.A. barrage, they cut straight across London at great height and top speed. They dropped several bombs in Central London.

Bomb hit one of London's oldest hospitals. Doctor was injured, but patients were safe in basement.

A New Zealand pilot who fought in the RAF explains why Britain survived the Battle of Britain (from *For Five Shillings a Day*, eds R Begg and P Liddle, 2002).

It wouldn't have survived if Hitler hadn't made the mistake of switching the attack away from the air-fields and concentrating on London; it gave the air-fields a breathing space and the aircrews time to get a little bit of sleep.

Make brief notes under the following headings:
- *Goering's strategy*
- *7 September 1940*
- *Postponement of Sealion*
- *Why Germany failed*

Questions

a What does Source A tell us about British morale in August 1940?

b Use Source B and your own knowledge to explain why this article was published in September 1940.

c How useful is Source C as evidence of the Battle of Britain? Use Source C and your own knowledge to answer this question.

d Is Source D a fair interpretation of why Hitler failed to defeat the RAF in 1940? Use Source D and your own knowledge to answer this question.

Key Issue

- Why did the Allies win the Battle of the Atlantic?

Britain in 1939 imported half its food and two-thirds of its **raw materials**. The Atlantic Ocean soon became a battleground as Britain fought to keep the seas safe for its **merchant ships** to bring in these vital supplies. The main threat came from German U-boats or submarines. Submarines were very small craft but each one of their 14 torpedoes could sink any ship afloat.

Germany's U-boat or submarine fleet was led by Admiral Doenitz but at the start of the war he had only 22 U-boats available for use in the Atlantic. The period 1940–1 was, nonetheless, very successful for the U-boats, especially as their numbers increased. In 1941 Britain only managed to import 26 million tonnes of supplies – compared with the 68 million tonnes needed in 1938. By January 1942 Doenitz had a U-boat fleet of 300.

ANTI-SUBMARINE METHODS

The British quickly adopted the **convoy** system of escorting merchant ships with anti-submarine warships called destroyers. Destroyers used an electronic listening device called sonar or asdic which detected the position of submerged U-boats. The destroyer then fired off several depth charges (underwater explosive devices). These were set to explode at a fixed depth. The pressure of the explosion could crush or split a submarine's hull but it had to be close enough – no more than nine metres away.

Submarines on the surface used diesel engines, but below the surface they could only use battery-powered electric motors. After a day, the air in the cramped quarters became unbreathable and they would have to surface. This is when they were most at risk from being spotted by aircraft and enemy ships.

From 1943 submarines weren't even safe at night. This was because the invention of centimetric radar allowed aircraft and ships to detect a surfaced submarine in the dark up to six kilometres away. They were then able to use a powerful searchlight equal to 80 million candles to pinpoint its precise position.

The Germans partly managed to get round this problem by using a snorkel pipe which reached the surface from periscope depth. This allowed in enough air to run the diesel engines below the water. But these weren't in use until early 1944, and by then it was too late to bring the U-boats victory in the 'Battle of the Atlantic'.

A SOURCE

'The Atlantic Gap' was a stretch of about 1000 km in the middle of the Atlantic which land-based aircraft could not reach. German submarines could operate safely in this area until May 1943.

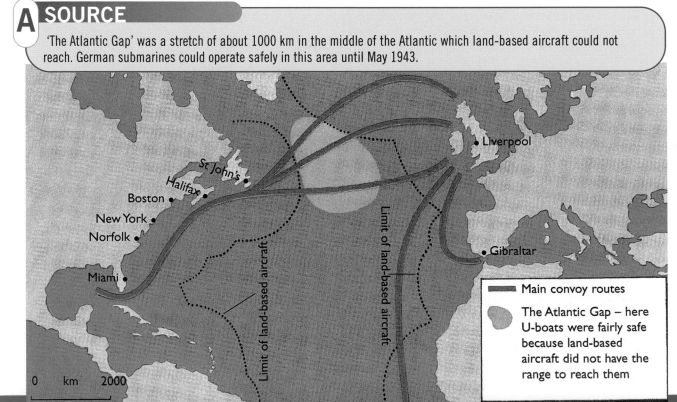

Main convoy routes

The Atlantic Gap – here U-boats were fairly safe because land-based aircraft did not have the range to reach them

Liverpool

St John's

Halifax

Boston

New York

Norfolk

Miami

Gibraltar

Limit of land-based aircraft

0   km   2000

'THE HAPPY TIMES'

Despite such anti-submarine methods, the U-boat threat was extremely serious. Doenitz ordered his submarines to attack in large groups, or 'wolf packs', at night and on the surface where they could not be detected by sonar before 1943. This proved very effective, and Britain lost 1875 ships in 1940 and 1941 in the Atlantic – a quarter of Britain's merchant fleet. The German crews called these years 'the happy times'.

In December 1941 the USA entered the war and the 'happy times' of 1941 became even happier. The Americans decided against the convoy system and their merchant ships sailed unescorted, close to the east coast of the USA. At night the ships could be seen against the lights of the coastal cities and were easy prey for the U-boat packs of 15–20 submarines. The authorities were against a black-out because it would be bad for tourism! In May 1942 the Americans ordered a blackout on the east coast and began to organise convoy escorts for their merchant ships.

THE END OF THE 'U-BOAT PERIL'

Over six million tonnes of British and American shipping were sunk in 1942 (nearly 1200 ships), and by January 1943 the Royal Navy had only two months' supply of oil left. 'The only thing that ever really frightened me in the whole war,' wrote Churchill later, 'was the U-boat peril'. But by the end of 1943 the 'U-boat peril' had been beaten. It is worth pointing out, however, that the Battle of the Atlantic was not won by sheer weight of numbers or superiority of technology. The battle was won in 1943 before these could have an impact. The Atlantic Gap, for example, was closed by only 37 converted Liberators (long range aircraft) with the range to patrol the whole area.

The **Allies** built 14 million tonnes of new ships in 1943. U-boat losses became too high for the Germans – between August and December 1943 only 51 ships were sunk in the Atlantic in a year in which the Germans lost 237 submarines. Only 117 ships were sunk in the whole of 1944. The Germans built 1100 submarines during the war. Of these, 785 were sunk and 28,000 members of Germany's U-boat crews (72 per cent of the total) perished with them.

B SOURCE

British wartime poster.

A FEW
**CARELESS WORDS
MAY END IN THIS–**
Many lives were lost in the last war through careless talk
Be on your guard! Don't discuss movements of ships or troops

C SOURCE

Allied merchant ships sunk in the Atlantic, 1939–44 (from *The World War Two Databook*, J Ellis, 1993).

	Tonnes	Number of ships
1939	755,000	220
1940	3,650,000	1007
1941	3,300,000	875
1942	6,150,000	1170
1943	2,170,000	363
1944	500,000	117

D SOURCE

A British historian, David Syrett, on the Battle of the Atlantic (from *The Battle of the Atlantic*, Andrew Williams, 2002).

This was a battle the Germans might have won but ... they lost because of superior Allied strategy, tactics ... and technology.

Questions

a **What does Source A tell you about the Battle of the Atlantic?**

b **Why were posters like Source B distributed in Britain? Use Source B and your own knowledge to answer this question.**

c **How useful is Source C to an historian studying the Battle of the Atlantic?**

d **Is Source D an accurate interpretation of why the Allies won the Battle of the Atlantic? Use Source D and your own knowledge to answer this question.**

'When Barbarossa commences the world will hold its breath,' Hitler said of his bold plan to invade the Soviet Union. The scale of the campaign was certainly huge. Hitler assembled three million troops, 3500 tanks and 2700 aircraft for 'Operation Barbarossa' – the German code-name for the attack on Russia.

Hitler invaded the Soviet Union on 22 June 1941, ordering his troops to flatten Russia 'like a hailstorm'. The reasons for the invasion were a mixture of the military and the political. Hitler needed Russia's plentiful **raw materials** to support his army and population. There was oil in the Caucasus and wheat in the Ukraine.

He was also obsessed by racial ideas. The Russians, he believed, were an 'inferior' Slav race which would offer no real resistance to racially 'superior' Germans. Russia's fertile plains could provide even more ***Lebensraum*** (living space) than Poland. Russia was also the heart of world communism and Hitler detested **communists**.

The Russian army had done very badly during its brief war with Finland in the winter of 1939–40. This convinced Hitler that the Soviet Union and its Red Army could be beaten in four months. His confidence was also boosted by the fact that in the late 1930s, Stalin, the Soviet **dictator**, had shot 35,000 officers (43 per cent of all his officers) in the Red Army. Stalin believed that the army was plotting against him.

But the invasion of Russia was Hitler's biggest mistake of the war so far – especially with Britain still undefeated in the west. Germany was now committed to a war on two fronts. Hitler's arrogance and contempt for his enemies was to prove his most serious failing.

Hitler was confident that his army would match the Soviet army in size and would have much better equipment. For example, only 1500 of Russia's 10,000 tanks were capable of fighting the German tanks on equal terms.

The Russians were taken completely by surprise by the German invasion and fell back, trading men and territory for time. As they retreated they 'scorched the earth', destroying everything which could provide food or shelter for the Germans. This proved very serious for the Germans when winter set in.

The Germans captured tremendous numbers of Soviet troops – three million by the end of 1941. But Stalin made good the losses in men and materials. He had ordered some 1500 factories (80 per cent of Russia's industrial output) to be moved by rail far to the east, away from the fighting. Here, these factories were quickly in production once more. However many tanks the Germans destroyed or men they captured, they still seemed to face an endless supply of both.

BATTLES OF ENCIRCLEMENT

Hitler had three principal targets within the Soviet Union. Army Group North (AGN) was ordered to capture Leningrad, an important **armaments** industry centre; Army Group Centre (AGC) headed for the capital, Moscow; Army Group South (AGS) set out for the Ukraine.

Hitler believed that the French invasion of Russia in 1812 failed because they allowed the Russians to retreat. This drew the French deep into Russian territory and made it harder to keep their troops supplied. Hitler would stop the Russians retreating by getting behind the Soviet troops in 'battles of encirclement'. This would cut off their retreat and lead to the capture of large numbers of enemy troops. To some extent this worked, but the Russian army was not short of men.

Only AGS eventually took its objective. But by the end of 1941, it seemed only a matter of time before the Soviet Union would collapse. German troops were at the gates of Leningrad and only 60 kms (40 miles) from Moscow.

A SOURCE

A modern history book on the first day of the invasion (from *Stalingrad*, Antony Beevor, 1998).

German Air Force raids . . . over the next nine hours destroyed 1200 Soviet aircraft, the vast majority on the ground. German pilots could hardly believe their eyes when, banking over air bases, they glimpsed hundreds of enemy planes neatly lined up beside the runways. Those Soviet planes which managed to get off the ground . . . proved easy targets . . . their out-dated models stood no chance.

B SOURCE

A German pilot commenting on a raid on a Soviet airfield on the first day of the invasion (from *The War Years, 1939–45: Eyewitness Accounts*, 1994).

Then we dropped the bombs. The line of bombs continued along the length of the field and tore up the runway. No fighters would be able to take off from there for some time. I could see that about 15 of the Soviet fighter aircraft on the runway were in flames. We had been so successful that there was no longer any need to carry out the second raid we had planned on the airfield.

C SOURCE

A modern history book on the start of the German invasion (from *Russia's War*, R Overy, 1997).

So convinced had Stalin been that Germany would not attack in the summer that even the most basic of precautions were lacking. Aircraft were lined up in inviting rows at the main air bases, uncamou-flaged. At least 1200 of them were destroyed within hours of the war's beginning, most of them on the ground.

D SOURCE

Soviet poster from 1943 shows Soviet civilians being executed by the Nazis. The text reads 'Our hope is in you, Red Warrior'.

ВСЯ НАДЕЖДА НА ТЕБЯ, КРАСНЫЙ ВОИН

Questions

a What can you learn from Source A about the Soviet Air Force in June 1941?

b Does Source C support the evidence of Sources A and B about the Soviet Air Force in the early days of the invasion?

c How useful are Sources D and E as evidence of German treatment of Soviet civilians?

d 'The German invasion was successful in 1941 because it was well-planned.' Use the sources and your own knowledge to explain whether you agree with this view.

E SOURCE

Bodies of Soviet civilians shot by the Germans in a schoolyard at Rostov-on-Don. The photograph was made public by the Russians in January 1942.

STALINGRAD

Hitler did not give up on the Caucasus oilfields. In the summer of 1942 he planned an offensive to capture Stalingrad. Stalin told the defenders of Stalingrad: 'Not a step back'. For five months, until January 1943, every room of every floor of every building was fought over. In one three-day period in September 1942 the railway station changed hands 15 times.

By the end of November the 300,000 Germans inside Stalingrad, under the command of General von Paulus, were cut off and surrounded by Russian forces commanded by General Zhukov. Paulus asked for permission to break out to save his army but Hitler refused. Eventually, the remaining 90,000 Germans, cut off and starving, were forced to surrender on 30 January 1943.

It was the biggest German defeat of the war so far. The Battle of Stalingrad was important for strategic reasons – the Germans could not now capture the Caucasus oilfields. But its real importance lay in the boost it gave to Soviet (and **Allied**) morale. The German army could be beaten.

KURSK: OPERATION CITADEL

The only significant attempt by the Germans to stop the Russian advance after Stalingrad was at Kursk. Hitler code-named this, the biggest battle of the entire war, 'Operation Citadel'.

The Battle of Kursk (5–16 July 1943), in the words of Richard Overy, 'tore the heart out of the German army'. German and Russian losses in men and machines were huge, but the difference was that the Russians could replace both easily. In August 1943 the Germans had just 2500 tanks on the whole of the Eastern Front while the Soviet Union had 8200.

Stalingrad and Kursk were the two decisive battles on the Eastern Front. The German siege of Leningrad ended in January 1944 when the Russians relieved the city. It had lasted 900 days and cost at least 800,000 civilian lives. By December the Soviet Red Army was ready to invade Germany itself.

WHY DID BARBAROSSA FAIL?

Hitler expected to capture most of Russia's factories in the early stages of the war, and this would have made sure of a German victory. But Russia was able to make up its losses in tanks and planes because Stalin had managed to move over 1500 factories out of the range of the Germans.

But there were other reasons too. Hitler's over-confidence also led him to invade without preparing for a winter campaign. The war would be over before the winter, Hitler claimed. The Soviet forces were much better equipped for this. The Germans, starved and exposed to the cold by the 'scorched earth' policy (see Chapter 8) simply froze.

The German generals liked to claim after the war that they lost simply because the Russians had more of everything – tanks, planes and men – but this misses the importance of the tremendous courage and patriotism of the Soviet troops. Hitler's racial theories could not accept that Slav 'sub-humans' could display such qualities.

German brutality towards the Soviet civilians they controlled also worked against them. As a result, many civilians joined the 250,000 or so **resistance** fighters. It is possible that many of the peoples of the Soviet Union, such as the Ukrainians, would have accepted German rule in place of communism – if the Germans had treated them well.

The Red Army had taken on 75 per cent of Germany's military power and won, and could justly claim to have done the most to defeat Hitler. The Soviet army eliminated no fewer than 607 German divisions with six million Germans killed, wounded or captured. The British and Americans together defeated just 176 divisions.

A SOURCE

A modern historian describes the effects of the cold on the Germans (from *Barbarossa*, Alan Clark, 1965).

Many of the men were without any clothing to add to their uniforms except denim combat overalls. These they used to pull on over their uniforms and . . . fill the loose folds with screwed-up paper. The impact of the cold was made worse by the complete absence of shelter; the ground was impossibly hard to dig, and most of the buildings had been destroyed in the fighting.

B SOURCE

German soldiers, captured by the Russians, on the Eastern Front.

C SOURCE

A description by a modern historian of how German troops tried to cope with the effects of the Russian winter (from *Stalingrad*, Antony Beevor, 1998).

Many soldiers had still not received proper winter clothing so they tried make their own with varying degrees of success. Under their uniforms, more and more of them wore articles of Soviet uniform – buttonless tunic shirts and baggy quilted trousers and the highly-prized quilted jackets. In hard frosts, a steel helmet became like a freezer compartment, so they wore scarves and even Russian foot bandages wrapped round their heads as insulation.

D SOURCE

Two Russian specialist soldiers (snipers) in winter camouflage uniforms.

E SOURCE

Weapons production in 1941 (from *Russia's War*, Richard Overy, 1997).

	Aircraft	Tanks	Artillery
USSR	15,735	6590	42,300
Germany	11,766	5200	7000

Questions

a What can you learn from Source A about the conditions for German soldiers?

b Does Source C support the evidence of Sources A and B about the effect of the winter on the German troops?

c How useful are Sources D and E as evidence about why the Soviet Union defeated the Germans?

d 'The Germans' biggest mistake was their failure to prepare their troops for the winter cold.' Use the sources and your own knowledge to explain whether you agree with this view.

STRATEGIC BOMBING

There were two types of bombing in the Second World War: strategic bombing and tactical bombing. Tactical bombing is the use of aircraft to bomb targets as part of an attack by the navy or the army. Strategic bombing involves attacks on the enemy's factories and cities.

When war broke out, the Prime Minister at the time, Neville Chamberlain, ordered the RAF not to bomb Germany at all. He was afraid of provoking German raids on Britain. But Churchill had different ideas. He believed that strategic bombing was the only method Britain had of hitting back at Germany. He also faced a great deal of pressure from Stalin. Stalin had accused Britain of not doing enough in the fight against **Nazism** and Churchill had to offer something. He ordered the RAF's Bomber Command to launch an all-out bombing offensive over Germany. This was despite evidence from a British investigation in May 1942 which said that only 25 per cent of bombs dropped fell within eight kilometres of the target.

'BOMBER' HARRIS

Arthur Harris became the commander of the RAF's Bomber Command in February 1942. He firmly believed that the war could be won by intensive bombing of Germany's cities. From 1942 onwards, 'Bomber' Harris put his theories into practice – on Churchill's orders. In May 1942 he launched the first 1000-bomber raid over Germany, with Cologne the target. This one raid killed about 40,000 Germans, and a week-long raid over Hamburg in July and August 1943 killed 45,000.

About 750,000 German civilians perished as a result of the RAF's night-time, and the American day-time, raids over Germany's cities. This is far more than the 60,000 Britons killed by German raids.

It has been a matter of some controversy whether these raids really did help to defeat Germany. The historian, Richard Overy, has argued that the real success of the bombing offensive was that it forced the Germans to use valuable military resources (such as fighter planes) and men in defending their cities. In 1944, for example, one-third of all artillery pieces made were used as anti-aircraft guns. These guns would otherwise have been used against **Allied** tanks in France or Russia.

Arthur Harris, though, was ignored by Churchill at the end of the war. He was not made a lord, unlike the other war leaders, and there was no special medal for Bomber Command air crew. Harris was disgusted at this 'insult' and left England. It was not until 1995 that a statue was finally put up in his memory.

'From this British poster from 1940, it is clear that the RAF bombing campaign over Germany's cities devastated German industry.' Do the statistics in Source D support this claim?

A SOURCE

Arthur Harris, Commander in Chief of Bomber Command, addressed bomber crews in 1942 with these words.

It has been decided that the primary object of your operations should now be focused on the morale of the enemy civil population and, in particular, of the industrial workers ... We are bombing Germany city by city and ever more terribly in order to make it impossible for her to go on with the war.

B SOURCE

A modern historian writes about the Allied bombing campaign over Germany (adapted from *Total War*, P Calvocoressi, 1972).

In Berlin the damage was severe enough to cause many to leave the city and to close all the schools, but less than half of the city's industries stopped work and many of the stoppages were brief ... morale did not break in either Berlin or Hamburg. Bomber Command failed to bring German industry to a halt.

C SOURCE

A military historian, Brigadier Peter Young, on the impact of the Allied bombing of Germany (from *World War 1939–45*, Peter Young, 1966).

On October 14, 1943, 291 US Flying Fortresses set off to attack the greatest centre of German ball-bearing production. The Fortresses did severe damage but 60 were shot down. The strategic bombing offensive brought the German war economy almost to the point of collapse.

D SOURCE

Statistics of German industrial and military output from 1940–4 with industrial output (coal, steel, oil) shown in millions of tonnes.

	1940	1941	1942	1943	1944
Coal	268	315	318	340	348
Steel	21	28	29	31	26
Oil	5	6	7	8	5
Tanks	2200	5200	9200	17,300	22,100
Aircraft	10,200	11,800	15,400	24,800	39,800

E SOURCE

Photograph of Dresden, March 1946.

F SOURCE

A modern historian on the Allied bombing campaign (from *The Oxford Companion to the Second World War*, A N Frankland, 1995).

British Bomber Command and the Eighth USAAF [United States Army Air Force] did produce an oil famine in Germany, the collapse of its transport system and a fearful levelling of its great cities. These results were too late to win the war on their own, but they did make a decisive contribution to the defeat of Germany.

Questions

a What can you learn from Source A about the RAF's policy of bombing Germany?

b Does Source C support the evidence of Sources A and B about the effect of the Allied bombing of Germany?

c How useful are Sources D and E about the effectiveness of Allied bombing of Germany?

d 'The bombing of Germany had no significant impact on Germany's war effort.' Use the sources and your own knowledge to explain whether you agree with this view.

THE SECOND FRONT: JUNE 1944

Stalin repeatedly asked Churchill and Roosevelt (the President of the USA) to open a **Second Front** by invading German-occupied France. This, he calculated, would force the Germans to withdraw troops from the war against Russia to deal with the British and Americans in France.

Stalin had expected the invasion of France to take place in 1943, but Churchill insisted that the attack be postponed for a year. Churchill told Stalin that an invasion of Italy had to come first. This, he claimed, would force the Germans to draw troops away from France to defend Italy. This would make an attack on France later on less difficult. Stalin suspected that the British and Americans really wanted the Russians to carry on killing Germans for them while Britain and the USA did very little. Relations between the three **Allied** powers were very strained at this time.

'LET'S GO!'

Eventually, after much secret planning, General Eisenhower, the American commander of all the Allied forces, decided that the good weather expected for 6 June 1944 would last long enough for a seaborne invasion of France to take place. D-Day would be 6 June. (The 'D', by the way, stands for 'Day'. The French call it 'Le Jour-J'.) He gave the go-ahead for Operation Overlord with the simple instruction: 'Let's go!'.

The choice of the Normandy beaches took the Germans completely by surprise – there was no suitable port on the Normandy coast for the Allies to unload the huge amount of supplies and equipment they would need for an invasion. Therefore, the Germans – Field Marshall Rommel included – expected an attack across the shortest sea route to Calais.

Eisenhower encouraged this belief by setting up a pretend invasion force in South-East England, opposite the Calais area. The tanks were made of rubber and landing craft of wood. The tents were real and so were the smoking camp stoves, to make it easier for German **reconnaissance** aircraft to spot them. Meanwhile, in the real invasion area, west of Portsmouth, the camp fires used smokeless fuel and every effort was made to keep the area secret from the Germans.

MULBERRIES

What the Germans didn't know was that the Allies planned to bring their own 'ports' with them: a secret weapon called 'Mulberry'. These were artificial harbours which could be towed across the Channel, and onto which tanks, trucks and supplies could be unloaded. Even after the first landings had taken place, Hitler was convinced that Normandy was not the real invasion. He held back two nearby tank divisions (over 500 tanks) until it was too late. When he was ready to use them, the British, American and Canadian divisions had established a firm hold on French soil.

60,000 troops landed on the first day and within a week over 300,000 were in France. After three months the number had grown to two million men and 450,000 vehicles pitched against the 600,000 troops available to Hitler. A key factor in the successful invasion was that the Germans had fewer than 200 aircraft to use against the landings – compared with the 12,000 available to the Allies. From then

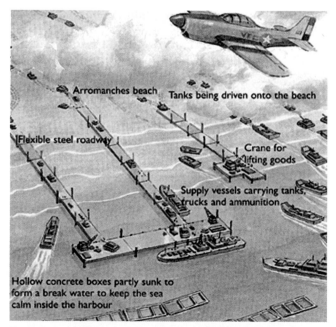

The Mulberry harbour was vital to the success of the Normandy Landings. Here can be seen the flexible steel roadways onto which the heavy trucks and tanks were unloaded.

onwards the Germans were gradually driven back towards Germany itself. Further bad news for Hitler arrived from Romania in August 1944. The Romanians changed sides, and abandoned their German allies. The Romanians had provided Germany with 23 per cent of its oil supplies, and now this was lost.

There were only two setbacks to the Allies' progress: Arnhem (September 1944) and the Ardennes Offensive (December 1944). At Arnhem, Montgomery's plan was to use airborne troops to seize vital bridges in Holland *behind* the German lines. These would be essential later for the invasion of northern Germany. But the reinforcements failed to fight their way through and the attack collapsed. The losses at one of the bridges at Arnhem were especially severe. Of the 10,000 troops used here 8000 were killed or captured.

ARDENNES OFFENSIVE

Hitler launched one last desperate counter-attack on the Belgian border in December to prevent an invasion of Germany itself. He used the last of his reserves and his fuel. At first, the Battle of the Bulge, as it is also known, was very successful as the Allies were taken completely by surprise. But because the Allies had more troops and far more aircraft they eventually broke the German offensive by the end of January 1945. By using these vital reserves in the west and not against the Russians, all Hitler had done was make it easier for the Red Army to conquer more of Germany – including Berlin.

In March 1945 the Allies crossed the Rhine into Germany from the west. In the following month the Russians took Berlin, the capital of Nazi Germany. Hitler shot himself on 30 April – two days after Mussolini had been executed by Italian **communist partisans**. Mussolini's body was left hanging upside down from a Milan garage. On 8 May Germany surrendered unconditionally. Hitler had boasted that **Nazism** would last 1000 years – 12 had proved more than enough.

A SOURCE

A modern historian on the air war over Normandy (from *Why the Allies Won*, Richard Overy, 1995).

On June 6th, against over 12,000 Allied aircraft, including 5600 fighters, the German Air Force could only use 170 working aircraft. Many of the aircraft sent were destroyed as Allied aircraft smashed German airfields in France. Many German pilots were plunged into the conflict before they were fully trained; many lost their way. The German reinforcements were shot out of the skies.

B SOURCE

German anti-invasion defences in the Calais area, 1944.

C SOURCE

A modern historian on how the Germans were deceived into thinking the invasion would take place in the Calais area (from *World War, 1939–45*, Peter Young, 1966).

The pre-D-Day bombing was so intense in the Pas de Calais that it did not betray the area selected for invasion.

D SOURCE

A modern historian on the importance of the invasion of Normandy (from *Why the Allies Won*, Richard Overy, 1995).

Hitler knew what was at stake in 1944. Defeat of the Allied invasion would amount to 'a turning point of the war', a psychological shock from which the British and American opinion would not recover.

Questions

a According to Source A, why were the Allies able to control the skies on D-Day?

b How useful is Source B to an historian studying the Allied invasion of Normandy in June 1944? Use Source B and your own knowledge to answer this question.

c Using Source C and your own knowledge, explain why the Germans were convinced the Allied invasion would be in the Calais area.

d 'An Allied defeat in June 1944 would have led to a German victory in the war.' Is this a fair interpretation? Use Source D and your own knowledge to answer this question.

Key Issue

- What was the key reason for the defeat of Germany?

INDUSTRY

A glance at the statistics in Source C suggests an easy answer to why Germany was defeated. The Germans lost because of the **Allies**' huge industrial power. This meant that the Allies could produce vast quantities of weapons and that they had the ability to keep these weapons going.

In August 1944 Romania quit the war and Germany lost 23 per cent of its oil supplies. Germany had so little oil left in 1944 that producing more tanks and planes would have been pointless anyway – they couldn't have moved. All of this suggests that Germany was doomed to lose the war – at least once the USA joined in. But overwhelming industrial power doesn't always lead to victory in war. The Germans in the first two years of the war easily out-produced Britain and the USSR in terms of steel production, yet this did not secure them a victory. The United States found this out 30 years later when it lost the Vietnam War. It is not enough to have more of everything. It is vital to have the will to win as well.

THE SOVIET ECONOMY

A key factor was the remarkable transformation of the Soviet and American economies.

Between July–December 1941 the Soviets moved 1500 entire factories from the path of the German invaders and re-assembled them well out of reach of the Germans. This remarkable achievement saved the Russians from certain defeat.

What the Russians could not evacuate they destroyed in the 'scorched earth' policy (see Chapter 8). Russia (and therefore Britain) came very close to defeat. In the year leading up to Stalingrad, Germany produced four times as much steel as Russia and so the balance of resources clearly favoured Germany.

However, the Russians, crucially, were able to produce more **armaments** with fewer **raw materials** than the Germans in 1943: 48,000 heavy guns and 27,000 tanks from 8m tons of steel and 90m tons of coal, compared with Germany's 24,000 guns and 17,000 tanks from 30m tons of steel and 340m tons of coal.

At first the Germans were able to win the support of considerable numbers of men within the countries they occupied. They were willing to join them in the fight against the **communist** *Soviet Union. Such men enlisted in the Waffen* **SS** *which was made up of foreigners fighting with the Germans. This poster reads 'You defend Belgium … fighting on the Eastern Front! Join the SS Armoured Walloon division.'*

This striking American poster from 1943 clearly gives one reason why the Allies were fighting – to save Christian civilisation from the evil of the Axis. The fact that the Allies believed, rightly, that they were fighting to free the world from a monstrous evil is an important factor in explaining their victory.

The Germans did not help themselves here with their insistence on producing finely engineered weapons, such as their tanks, which were difficult to mass-produce. The fact that they also produced so many different types of weapons also cut back production. The Germans made 42 different aircraft; the Soviets just five.

THE US ECONOMY

The most remarkable achievement of the American economy is not that in 1941 it produced more steel, oil, and motor vehicles than the rest of the world put together, but that it was able to transform itself into a *military* economy so quickly and with no real experience of large-scale military production. The US produced almost two-thirds of all Allied war production during the war, and as early as 1942 was already out-producing the **Axis** powers.

Henry J Kaiser transformed shipbuilding with a mass-production technique involving pre-fabricated parts. These 'Liberty Ships' could be built every 41 days as opposed to the previous 355. The motor industry was similarly transformed. In 1941 3.5m private cars had been built. After 1941 just 139 were made. This freed vast industrial capacity for the war effort. Henry Ford applied mass-production principles to bomber construction – thought to be impossible, given that a B-24 Liberator bomber required 1.5m parts. Yet Ford turned out a B-24 every 63 minutes.

ITALY

Hitler claimed he lost the war because the alliance with Italy diverted German troops away from the Eastern Front to the Mediterranean to help the Italians. But Germany never had more than 20 divisions operating in the Mediterranean during the war. The USA fought a three-front war, which was many thousands of kilometres from its shores and still won. However, this alliance did draw German forces into the Mediterranean when they should have been concentrating on Russia.

'BARBAROSSA' – THE BIGGEST MISTAKE

Certainly, the German invasion of Russia, 'Operation Barbarossa', was Hitler's biggest error. Here the Germans concentrated 75 per cent of their men, tanks, and aircraft and the Russians destroyed them. The Russians eliminated 600 German divisions compared to fewer than 180 destroyed by the Americans and British.

German ill-treatment of the people they conquered has also been put forward as a reason for their defeat. Chapters 8 and 9 on the war in Russia suggest that some of the Soviet peoples were ready to support Germany rather than communism but they soon turned against Germany. As many as 250,000 Soviet **partisans** fought the Germans behind their lines, tying down many troops. Similar **resistance** groups sprang up in Poland, France and Italy.

AIRCRAFT: THE KEY TO VICTORY

Historians, though, place much more importance on the industrial power of the British, Americans and Russians. This allowed the Allies to produce vast numbers of the most important weapon of the war: aircraft. The value of strategic bombing was not in the damage it inflicted on industry or morale, but in the way it forced the Germans to divert war production to the defence of German cities. For example, one-third of all artillery guns made in 1944 were used as anti-aircraft guns and not sent to the Eastern Front. Two-thirds of Germany's precious aircraft were used in the defence against bombing raids (and largely destroyed), so that German air defences against the Normandy Landings or on the Soviet Front were hopelessly ineffective. The historian, Richard Overy, has calculated that the combined effects of direct bombing and the use of military equipment to defend Germany's cities denied to German forces in France and Russia about half their battle-front weapons and equipment in 1944.

The tactical importance of air power is clear from the success of the Normandy landings. These were not bound to succeed by any means. For the first four or five weeks the Germans had sufficient forces to drive the Allies back into the sea – had they been used. The troops in Normandy were more experienced and tough and their equipment every bit as good as the Allies. But they had no air cover. One

German commander estimated that 50 per cent of his losses were caused by Allied bombers who flew without facing any opposition from German fighters. The Germans lost some 600,000 troops – killed, wounded or captured – in the loss of France in 1944. Defeat in France meant that Germany could not avoid losing the war.

A SOURCE

A German commander after the Normandy Landings (from *Why the Allies Won*, Richard Overy, 1995).

I cannot understand these Americans. Each night we know that we have cut them to pieces, inflicted heavy casualties, mowed down their transport. But – in the morning, we are suddenly faced with fresh troops, with complete replacements of men, machines, food, tools and weapons. This happens every day.

B SOURCE

German poster from 1944. The text reads 'Just as we fight – so will you work for victory!'

A comparison of German and Allied industrial and military production in 1994.

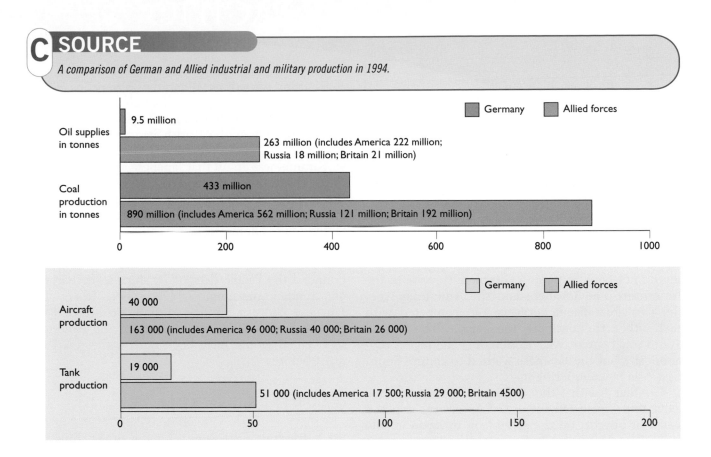

D SOURCE

The modern historian, Richard Overy, on why the Allies won the war (from *Why the Allies Won*, 1995).

The key to the eventual victory of the Allied states lies in the remarkable revival of Soviet military and economic power to a point where the Red Army could first contain, then drive out the German invader.

Make brief notes under the following headings:
- The Soviet economy
- The US economy
- Operation Barbarossa
- Air power

Questions

a What does Source A tell us about US military power at the time of the Normandy landings?

b Why was Source B distributed in Germany in 1944? Use Source B and your own knowledge to answer this question.

c How useful is Source C to an historian studying the reasons for Germany's defeat? Use Source C and your own knowledge to answer this question.

d Is Source D an accurate interpretation of why Germany lost the war? Use Source D and your own knowledge to answer this question.

13 THE WAR IN THE PACIFIC

Key Issue

Why were the Americans taken by surprise?

The Japanese attack on the American naval base at Pearl Harbor in the middle of the Pacific Ocean should not have come as a complete surprise to the Americans. The Japanese and the Americans were the two great Pacific powers and competed with each other to dominate the region. The United States was content with dominating the region economically, but the Japanese wanted to control South East Asia by conquering it.

Conflict with the United States seemed inevitable – especially after the Americans imposed a ban or boycott on the sale of oil to Japan in July 1941. The Americans imposed the boycott because Japan had invaded China in 1937. This was a severe blow to the Japanese economy since they depended on the USA for two-thirds of their oil supplies.

The military leaders realised that Japan could never dominate South East Asia unless it controlled its own supplies of vital **raw materials** like oil, rubber, iron ore and rice. These could only be acquired through war. If Japan was to stand any chance in a war against the USA it would have to strike first with a devastating blow. They chose the American Pacific Fleet at Pearl Harbor in Hawaii as the target.

PEARL HARBOR

American intelligence had cracked the Japanese secret code. They knew that an attack against the United States was planned – only they were not sure where. It was assumed the target would be the Philippines and not Pearl Harbor.

If war broke out, the American commander of the Pacific Fleet, Admiral Kimmel, was under orders to prepare to attack the Japanese Marshall Islands. These were 3250 kilometres to the *south west* of Pearl Harbor. This was the area which Kimmel kept an eye on with the three **reconnaissance** planes he had. But the Japanese attack, when it came, came from the *north* and Kimmel was taken completely by surprise.

Kimmel didn't think Pearl Harbor could be attacked by torpedoes dropped by planes because the water in the harbour wasn't deep enough for them. So he removed the nets which protected the

ships from torpedoes. What the Americans didn't know was that the Japanese had changed their torpedoes to run in shallow water. These were the same type of torpedoes the British had used against the Italian fleet 13 months earlier.

Kimmel was afraid that Japanese agents in Hawaii might try sabotage against Pearl Harbor's aircraft. So these were grouped together to make it easier to guard them. When the Japanese fleet sailed undetected 5500 kilometres across the Pacific to within 450 kilometres of Hawaii, the Americans were looking elsewhere. Two waves of Japanese aircraft pounded the Pacific fleet of 70 ships in its harbour on Sunday morning, 7 December 1941. The Japanese chose a Sunday morning to attack Pearl Harbor because they knew many of the American servicemen would have been out on the town the night before.

CARRIERS ESCAPE!

Six battleships were sunk plus ten other ships and 164 planes destroyed. 2400 servicemen and civilians also died. However, though the damage was devastating, it was not as great as the Japanese had hoped. The American aircraft carriers – a key target – were out on manoeuvres that morning.

Furthermore, the Japanese commander, Nagumo, decided not to attack the ship repair facilities or the oil storage units. This meant that the damaged vessels could be repaired quickly and that the fleet would have the fuel to hit back – when it was ready. But that would not be for another six months.

In the long term, Pearl Harbor was not a success for the Japanese. The attack enraged American public opinion because it came before an official declaration of war.

A SOURCE

On 6 December, the day before Pearl Harbor was attacked, an American intelligence official decoded a top secret Japanese message. This extract outlines events. (adapted from *Infamy*, J Toland, 1982).

The message was shown to President Roosevelt, who said: 'This means war'. Even so, no warning was sent to Hawaii where the Pacific Fleet was based. In fact, no Japanese decoded messages had been sent to the fleet's commander, Admiral Kimmel, for months . . . Several of these men urged that Kimmel . . . be warned but for some reason their superiors would not allow this.

B SOURCE

Map of the Pacific at the time of the Japanese attack.

Japan

Route of Japanese Fleet

Attack launched 450 km from Pearl Harbor, Hawaii

Pearl Harbor

Philippines (US expected attack here)

Marshall Islands

Area under surveillance by US Pacific Fleet aircraft at Pearl Harbor

Borneo

New Guinea

Australia

C SOURCE

The Oxford Companion to the Second World War (ed. I C B Dear, 1995) on the attack at Pearl Harbor.

Admiral Kimmel had no idea where the Japanese carriers were . . . Kimmel's dilemma was a real one. In the event of war, he was required to raid the Japanese Marshall Islands, which meant he had to keep aircraft in reserve for long-range reconnaissance of them . . . It was here that the only three reconnaissance aircraft were patrolling. But the Japanese approached from the north.

D SOURCE

Photograph of a blazing US ship at Pearl Harbor, 7 December 1941.

E SOURCE

United States poster, 1942.

F SOURCE

Historian William Manchester on the attack at Pearl Harbor (adapted from *Goodbye Darkness*, 1979).

US commanders in Hawaii and the Philippines were told '. . . an aggressive move by Japan is expected in the next few days'. Admiral Kimmel at Pearl Harbor decided to take no precautions. So officers and men were given their usual Saturday evening off on December 6. Only 195 of the navy's 780 anti-aircraft guns in the harbour were manned. And most of them lacked ammunition. It had been returned to storage because it tended to 'get dusty'.

Questions

a What can you learn from Source A about the Japanese attack on Pearl Harbor in December 1941?

b Does Source C support the evidence of Sources A and B about the attack on Pearl Harbor?

c How useful are Sources D and E as evidence about the effects of the attack on Pearl Harbor?

d 'Admiral Kimmel was to blame for the disaster at Pearl Harbor.' Use the sources and your own knowledge to explain whether you agree with this view.

14 THE DEFEAT OF JAPAN

→ **Key Issue**

Why did the Japanese lose the war?

JAPAN'S GAMBLE

Countries lose wars for a variety of reasons. Poor equipment, morale, and strategies can play a part, as can lack of industrial resources. The Japanese knew very well that they couldn't match the huge industrial resources of the United States, but the military leaders who led Japan into war didn't think this would matter. Their plan was simple. A surprise attack would allow Japan to conquer so much of the Pacific that the United States would be forced to negotiate a treaty. The Americans, the Japanese believed, would not have the stomach for the kind of casualties involved in a full-scale war to get these territories back.

However, this was a massive gamble because if the Japanese got the American response wrong they would surely lose the war. Japan's **raw material** resources were totally inadequate for a modern war. It depended on imports for 80 per cent of its iron ore and oil supplies. It had no bauxite (essential for electric cables and explosives) or rubber (essential for tyres).

SHORTAGES

The people of Japan had no particular enthusiasm for war but they were excited by the early victories. The government could keep morale up at first because Japan was winning. Later, it kept news of defeats like Midway secret. But Japan could only keep the effect of defeats from the population for a time. Rationing gradually became more severe as Japan's already small merchant fleet was sunk by American submarines and supplies became desperately short.

The Japanese never really grasped the importance of the submarine as an economic weapon. This was one which could be used against an enemy's supplies by attacking its merchant fleet. Japan's small submarine fleet was used more and more to keep its faraway garrisons in the Pacific supplied. This became more of a problem because of MacArthur's 'island hopping' strategy. Isolated garrisons, bypassed by the fighting, still had to be kept fed. These submarines would have been better used attacking American **merchant ships**.

In 1941, Japan had to import two million tonnes of rice to feed its population, but in 1944 it could only manage to import 650,000 tonnes. This was because 85 per cent of its merchant ships were sunk during the war. American bomber raids also helped to bring home to the population that Japan was losing the war. By February 1944 even the military leaders realised the war was lost.

A SOURCE

A comparison of levels of raw materials production for Japan and the United States in 1937 (from *The World War II Databook*, J Ellis, 1993).

	Coal	Oil	Iron ore	Copper	Wheat
USA	Exports	Exports	Self-sufficient	Exports	Self-sufficient
JAPAN	Not self-sufficient	Deficient	Not self-sufficient	Deficient	Not self-sufficient

Note:
- 'exports' means that the country had enough for its own needs and was able to export the rest for sale abroad;
- 'self-sufficient' means that the country had enough for its own needs but didn't have any left to sell abroad;
- 'not self-sufficient' means that the country did not have enough for its own needs;
- 'deficient' means that the country had no useful supplies at all of this raw material.

SOURCE

Table showing how various raw materials were used (from *The World War II Databook*, J Ellis, 1993).

RAW MATERIAL	USES
Coal	fuel for power stations, iron and steel furnaces; used in TNT for explosives
Oil	tank, truck, ship and aircraft fuel
Iron ore	needed for manufacture of steel – used in tanks, ships, aircraft, shells, weapons etc
Copper	electric wires and cables; cartridges and shells
Wheat	bread

SOURCE

A comparison of Japanese and American military production for 1944 (from *The World War II Databook*, J Ellis, 1993).

	Japan	United States
Aircraft	28,000	96,000
Machine-guns	380,000	2,700,000
Aircraft carriers	5	45

SOURCE

An American poster, 1944.

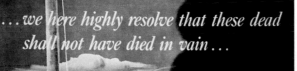

... we here highly resolve that these dead shall not have died in vain ...

REMEMBER DEC. 7th!

SOURCE

Effects of American bombing raids over Japan's five major cities between March and May, 1945 (from *The Experience of World War II*, ed. J Campbell, 1989).

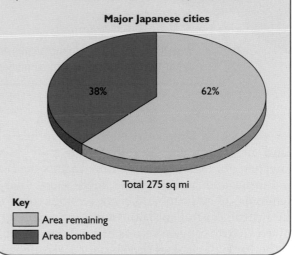

Major Japanese cities

38%   62%

Total 275 sq mi

Key
- Area remaining
- Area bombed

SOURCE

A modern historian comments on how spread out Japanese troops were in 1945 (adapted from *The Rise and Fall of the Great Powers*, Paul Kennedy, 1988).

Even when American forces were closing in on Japan in early 1945, and its cities were being smashed from the air, there were still one million Japanese soldiers in China and another 780,000 or so in Manchuria and these could not be moved to help defend Japan.

Questions

a What can you learn from Source A about why Japan was defeated in the war?
b Does Source C support the evidence of Sources A and B about why Japan was defeated?
c How useful are Sources D and E as evidence of why Japan was defeated?
d 'Japan was defeated because it could not produce enough weapons.' Use the sources and your own knowledge to explain whether you agree with this view.

Make brief notes under the following headings:
- Japan's gamble
- Raw material problems
- Shortages

15 AMERICAN VICTORY

→

Key Issue

- Was the dropping of atomic bombs on Japan necessary to get it to surrender?

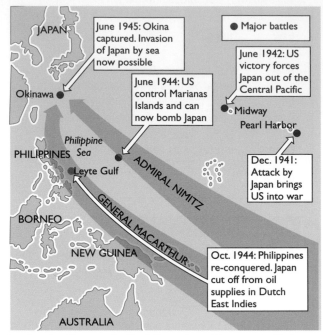

American land forces under MacArthur and naval forces under Nimitz planned to advance on Okinawa. From here they could invade Japan.

For six months after Pearl Harbor, Japan had a free hand in the Pacific and in South East Asia. It launched attacks at the same time against the British in Burma and Malaya. Here there were vital **raw materials**: oil and rubber. Japanese troops rolled back the British, Australians and Americans as victory followed victory. Singapore was Britain's key naval base in the Far East. Its loss in February 1942 along with 62,000 prisoners was a huge blow to morale.

The spectacular run of Japanese victories came to an end with the Battle of Midway in June 1942. The loss of four Japanese aircraft carriers proved to be devastating because Japan managed to build only another seven in the next two years. In the same time the United States built 90.

The Americans took command of the **Allied** campaign in the Pacific. The Americans developed an 'island hopping' or 'leap-frogging' strategy. This was similar to Hitler's ***Blitzkrieg*** in that strongly defended enemy islands were bypassed and isolated from support and reinforcements.

The re-conquest of the Philippines by General MacArthur, commander of the US troops in the Pacific area, in 1944 cut off Japan from its oil supplies in the Dutch East Indies. The loss of 60 million barrels of oil a year was a crushing blow. Japan could produce only two million barrels of its own.

The United States' Pacific progress, nonetheless, proved to be costly. Japanese resistance was fanatical. The warrior code of bushido taught that capture in battle was shameful. Japanese soldiers, therefore, preferred to fight to the death. Iwo Jima, a tiny volcanic island, was defended by 23,000 Japanese troops. Of these, 22,000 fought to the death rather than surrender. It was this kind of devotion to their Emperor, Hirohito, which so worried the Americans. What would American casualties be like when they had to attack Japan itself – and not tiny islands thousands of kilometres away?

The capture of Okinawa took place in June 1945 after two months of vicious fighting. 13,000 American soldiers and sailors had died to capture an island 550 kilometres from Japan itself. From here an invasion of mainland Japan could at last be launched – but at what cost to the United States?

THE ATOMIC BOMB

On 6 August the Americans dropped the world's first atomic bomb on Hiroshima and followed it three days later with another on Nagasaki. These two bombs killed over 200,000 people between them, many dying months later from the effects of radiation. The day after the bombing of Nagasaki, 10 August, Japan agreed to surrender.

It is generally assumed that the bombs forced Japan to surrender. Recent evidence suggests otherwise. After all, the American fire-bombing of Tokyo on one night in March 1945 had killed 85,000 civilians and the government of Japan fought on. Civilian casualties, therefore, were probably not an issue.

It is true that American lives were saved because a full-scale invasion of Japan was not needed, but this was not because of the two atomic bombs. Japan agreed to surrender because President Truman dropped the United States' demand for **unconditional surrender**. The Japanese would surrender, they said, if Emperor Hirohito were allowed to stay on the throne.

Truman agreed to this one condition and the war was over. He could have agreed to it before the bombing, but then the awesome power of the weapon would not have been proved. By demonstrating it, the United States delivered a timely warning to the Soviet Union not to cause problems with the Western powers after the war.

A SOURCE

Two American historians, Ernest and Trevor Dupuy, comment on the effect of the atomic bombs on the war (from *The Collins Encyclopedia of Military History*, 1993).

No one knows how long a fanatical ... Japan could have continued the war if the bombs had not been dropped. It is clear, however, that these weapons, combined with Soviet entry into the war, convinced the Japanese emperor and government that further resistance was hopeless.

B SOURCE

The British historian, Richard Overy, on the effect of the atomic weapons (from *Why the Allies Won*, 1995).

Atomic weapons did not win the war, for they came too late to decide who would win. Japan was on the point of surrender by the time the two available bombs were used ... The war was won with tanks, aircraft, artillery and submarines, the weapons with which it was begun.

C SOURCE

From a school textbook, *The USA, 1917–1980* (Nigel Smith, 1996).

Some US advisors said the bomb should be dropped somewhere relatively harmless, as a warning to Japan. Recent research supports the view that Japan may have been willing to surrender before Truman gave the orders to drop the new bombs.

D SOURCE

Evening News front page, dated 8 August 1945.

E SOURCE

Photograph of Hiroshima, taken September 1945.

F SOURCE

The historian, Philip Knightley, on the use of the atomic bombs on Japan (from *Truth the First Casualty*, 1975).

The success of the United States Navy in denying Japan her vital oil supplies is told in one simple table of figures. The following amounts of oil reached Japan from the areas she had conquered: in 1942, 40%; in 1943, 15%; in 1944, 5%; in 1945, none. With or without the atomic bomb ... Japan was finished, because her ships, aircraft, tanks, and vehicles could not move. They had no fuel.

Questions

a What can you learn from Source A about why Japan surrendered in 1945?

b Does Source C support the evidence of Sources A and B about why Japan surrendered in 1945?

c How useful are Sources D and E as evidence about the effect of the atomic bombing of Hiroshima?

d 'The use of the atomic bombs against Japan was unnecessary.' Use the sources and your own knowledge to explain whether you agree with this view.

Key Issue

• How did the government use propaganda and censorship during the war?

When war broke out in September 1939 the mood of the British people was not enthusiastic. The feeling was more one of 'let's get it over with'. A Canadian poet, Milton Acorn, wrote these lines in 1939:

This is where we came in; this has happened before
Only the last time there was cheering.

The 'last time', of course, was the First World War of 1914–18. The population did cheer when war broke out in 1914 but not this time. The government, though, was better prepared for war in 1939. Air Raid Precautions (ARP) had begun in 1938 and there were 100,000 **air-raid wardens** ready for duty. **Conscription** had been started in April 1939 – five months before the war started.

MASS OBSERVATION

The British public's reluctance to fight another war seemed justified as defeat followed defeat. It was the job of the government to keep up morale and to keep a check on it. **Mass Observation** was an organisation whose members reported conversations they overheard in pubs, shops and elsewhere. They also interviewed members of the public about specific issues to do with the war. The Ministry of Information used these reports to keep in touch with the public mood.

The King and Queen are seen here in Buckingham Palace after some of its outer buildings were damaged by a German air raid in September 1940. Churchill was quick to see the propaganda value of the raid – he ordered the attack to be given maximum publicity.

Sometimes these reports were very critical of the government's efforts to keep up morale. After the fall of France in June 1940, public morale was very low and Mass Observation blamed the government's poor efforts over propaganda. Government propaganda, it said, failed to lift the spirits of the people because it was written by upper class people who didn't understand how ordinary people spoke or felt.

The Ministry of Information (MoI) was the government department responsible for keeping the public informed about their duties and for maintaining their support for the war. It decided from the start to avoid exaggerating victories. This was easy to do when the news was mostly bad until late 1942. It would also avoid playing down defeats. The MoI would try to get across the truth and not give the public false hopes of early victory. This was a sensible approach, but the Ministry's early efforts were generally feeble and the public response was poor.

FIFTH COLUMNISTS

British poster propaganda was at its best when it appealed to the humour of the British people. Source C, from the MoI, shows one of a series of posters designed to stop people carelessly giving away military information to spies. The posters were popular and effective. There was a general worry that large numbers of German spies or British Nazi sympathisers, known as **Fifth Columnists**, were at work in Britain, listening in on careless conversations. However, all German spies in Britain were arrested and some became double-agents, working for British intelligence. The government also urged members of the public to inform on people making **defeatist** comments. This campaign was not popular and it created a tense and suspicious atmosphere. Churchill ordered it to be stopped.

INTERNMENT: 'COLLAR THE LOT!'

After the outbreak of the war, the government put into operation its plan for the **internment** of enemy citizens or 'aliens'. There were three categories. Category A was for those who were a serious threat and had to be interned. Those who were not interned but needed to be monitored were put in category B. Finally, there were those put in category C who were considered loyal to Britain and were allowed full liberty. By the end of November 1939 the government tribunals had listened to the cases of 74,000 Germans and Austrians living in Britain. Of these, 64,000 were placed in category C – many were Jews and anti-Nazis who had fled from Hitler

and only 600 were interned. However, by June 1940, this had crept up to 12,000 as the threat of a German invasion became more real. Women aliens were now also interned.

When Italy declared war on Britain in June 1940 Churchill decided to move immediately against the 20,000 Italians living in Britain. He ordered them all to be arrested: 'Collar the lot!'. By the middle of July, the number of interned Italians and Germans stood at 27,000. By the summer of 1941, the Fifth Columnist scare had died down and only 5000 committed Nazis and **fascists** were still in internment camps.

THE BBC

The British Broadcasting Corporation (BBC) played a key role in broadcasting propaganda to **Allied** and neutral countries, guided by the Ministry of Information. Broadcasts to enemy and occupied countries were organised by the Political Warfare Executive. The BBC was not under government control but it knew what it could or could not say in its news broadcasts. The BBC gained a reputation at

Germans were not allowed to listen to foreign radio broadcasts, in this case from London and Moscow. Those who did were labelled traitors – 'Verrater'. One of the phrases in the spiral of words coming from the foreign microphone is Soldatensender – the name of the PWE's propaganda broadcast to Germany.

home and abroad for reasonably honest reporting of the war and this is what made it such an effective propaganda tool. So important was the BBC that the government feared that if the Germans invaded Britain they would set up false BBC broadcasts to fool the British public. So, all BBC news readers were told to give their names when they read the news so that the public would get to know them and quickly spot impostors.

The BBC kept up civilian morale with popular entertainment programmes, such as the comedy, 'ITMA' (It's That Man Again) and the morale of the troops with 'Sincerely Yours' in which Vera Lynn sang songs requested by troops abroad. Eight million workers listened to 'Music While You Work' to help improve production.

CENSORSHIP

The case of J B Priestley, however, shows that sometimes the BBC forgot what could or could not be said. Priestley was a very popular broadcaster on the BBC with sometimes as many as 20 million Britons listening to him. Priestley sometimes criticised the government for not making the rich do more to help with the war and suggested that their empty homes should be used to house those whose homes had been bombed. The Ministry of Information, possibly on Churchill's orders, told the BBC to take him off the air and he was removed.

In general, **censorship** in Britain was mild. The press and radio were not allowed to mention the movement of troops, warships, and aircraft. Neither was the press allowed to show photographs of those killed by enemy bombing. The reports of war correspondents were censored to make sure that they contained nothing useful to the enemy. Similarly, private letters written by soldiers to their families were read by their officers for the same reason. Censored sentences were crossed out with thick blue pencils.

A SOURCE

An account of how the Ministry of Information dealt with the news that Buckingham Palace was bombed in September 1940 (from *A People's War*, Peter Lewis, 1986).

The Ministry of Information, with its genius for missing propaganda opportunities, was busy covering up news of the Palace bombing when Churchill heard of it: 'Dolts, idiots, fools!' he is said to have exploded. 'Spread the news at once! Let it be broadcast everywhere. Let the people of London know that the King and Queen are sharing the perils with them.'

BLACK PROPAGANDA

The Political Warfare Executive (PWE) was a government department which had the job of sending 'black propaganda' to the Germans. This type of propaganda involves the use of lies and trickery to undermine the morale of the enemy or confuse them. The PWE was particularly imaginative, but it is hard to say how successful its ideas were. Among its activities was the operation of a secret radio transmitter.

About 90 per cent of what the PWE broadcast was true, giving accurate details of German victories and Allied defeats. The broadcasters claimed they were anti-Nazi Germans inside the German army but their reports were also anti-British. Broadcasters even described Churchill as 'that flat-footed bastard of a drunken old Jew'. This helped to convince Germans that the broadcast could not be British. Occasionally, an invented item would be slipped into the reports.

One example was when a PWE broadcast informed German servicemen of the names of German streets destroyed in a bombing raid the previous evening. These men were told that if they lived in one of these streets they could get special leave to visit their families. Of course, when they applied for permission to visit them they were told no leave was possible. This, the PWE hoped, would anger them and lower the morale of the German servicemen.

B SOURCE

'Careless Talk Costs Lives'; a propaganda poster by the British artist, Fougasse.

you never know who's listening!

CARELESS TALK COSTS LIVES

This photograph, from January 1943, shows the bodies of young children being laid out in the playground after their school was bombed. The photograph was banned by the censors.

D SOURCE

An assessment of the role of the BBC by a modern historian (from *The Experience of World War Two*, ed. J Campbell, 1989).

The most useful propaganda weapon was the reputation which the British Broadcasting Corporation earned for its truthful reporting of news. It did not minimise British defeats, nor deliberately exaggerate British victories.

Make brief notes under the following headings:
- Mass Observation
- Ministry of Information
- Internment
- Role of the BBC
- Censorship

Questions

a According to Source A, why was Churchill so angry with the Ministry of Information?

b Why was Source C censored by the government? Use Source C and your own knowledge to answer this question.

c How useful is Source B to an historian studying Britain during the war? Use Source B and your own knowledge to answer this question.

d Is Source D an accurate interpretation of the importance of the BBC during the war? Use Source D and your own knowledge to answer this question.

17 THE BLITZ

Key Issue

- What was life like during the Blitz?

Until the end of August 1940 both sides in the war avoided bombing civilian targets. The RAF did bomb industrial areas, such as the Ruhr in Germany, in May and June of 1940 but the first RAF bombs did not fall on Berlin until the night of 24–25 August 1940. Hitler was so outraged by this raid that he immediately ordered Goering, the commander of the *Luftwaffe*, to begin **reprisal** raids on London. The first of these was on 7 September and began what became known as 'the Blitz' – the heavy German air-raids over Britain's cities. This lasted until May 1941.

At first, London was the only target. It was bombed for 76 nights in a row from 7 September. But in November the Germans added Coventry and other cities, such as Liverpool, Plymouth and Birmingham, to their list of targets. Coventry was a particular target because of the aircraft factories there.

At first there was little London's air defences could do against the raids. Searchlights at this time were not effective at altitudes above 3600 metres and so the German bombers simply flew above this height. RAF night fighters scored few successes. In one particularly heavy raid on 15 October the RAF managed to shoot down just one of the 400 bombers involved.

From February 1941 the Germans' main targets were the ports in the west of Britain. These were the main ports for supplies from the United States. Between February–May 1941, 46 raids were made against ports such as Plymouth, Swansea, Belfast and Portsmouth, while London was bombed only seven times.

THE HOME GUARD

In May 1940 the government hurriedly set up the Local Defence Volunteers to deal with the possibility of a German invasion by parachutists. They were a second line of defence, consisting of men too young or too old to serve in the regular army. Their job was to patrol through the night to warn of any parachute landings. By June there were nearly 1.5 million of them.

Churchill suggested they change their names to the Home Guard but they still remained a figure of fun and were called 'Dad's Army'. At first, they had no guns or uniforms and paraded with broomsticks. They placed bed frames and old buses in fields to stop German gliders from landing. By 1942 the Home Guard was properly trained and equipped and numbered nearly two million.

THE BAEDEKER RAIDS

There were few raids after May 1941 until April 1942 when German planes bombed historic cities such as Exeter, York and Bath. These attacks were in revenge for RAF raids over German historic cities in March.

One German spokesman described the attacks on these old English cities as 'Baedeker raids'. Baedeker was the name of a tourist guide to famous cities of cultural interest. The phrase was a propaganda disaster for the Germans because it implied they really were barbarians with no respect for culture.

THE SECOND BLITZ

In the middle of 1944 Hitler launched the first of his secret 'Vengeance' weapons – the V-1. Hitler was determined to pay back the **Allies** for their 'terror' bombing of German cities. The V-1 was a rocket-powered flying bomb which had no pilot. After flying a fixed number of kilometres, the engine cut out and the rocket crashed to the ground.

The V-1 was difficult but not impossible to shoot down. The sound of its droning engine and then the terrible silence as it cut out brought terror to Londoners for the last nine months of the war. Just over 10,000 were launched against England but only 3500 of these found a target, killing 6200 people. The rest were shot down or crashed before reaching the coast.

The next terror weapon was the V-2. It carried only a slightly bigger explosive load (1000 kilograms) than the V-1. But, unlike the V-1, the V-2 could not be stopped since it was a rocket which reached a speed of 4000 kilometres per hour before impact. It exploded without warning. From September 1944 until the end of March 1945 an average of five a day fell on England, killing nearly 3000 civilians. These were powerful weapons but it is worth noting that the RAF's Lancaster bombers were able to drop bombs with 5400 kilograms of explosives over Germany from June 1944.

A SOURCE

A London woman's account of sleeping in an underground station during the Blitz (from *A People's War*, Peter Lewis, 1986).

If you got in too late you would have to sit up straight with nothing to lean against. Most people somehow found room to lie down for some part of the night but I doubt if anyone got more than two or three hours sleep. They had to leave one yard clear for genuine travellers to get on and off the trains and they were quite good about that.

B SOURCE

Londoners sleeping in an underground station in 1940.

D SOURCE

Ministry of Home Security report on the situation in Portsmouth during the Blitz (adapted from *The Ministry of Morale*, I McClaine, 1979).

On all sides we hear that looting has reached an alarming level. The police seem unable to keep control. This seems another example of the lack of community spirit. The effect on morale is bad and there is a general feeling of desperation as there seems to be no solution.

Questions

a According to Source A, what was it like sleeping in an underground station?

b Look at Source B. Why were so many Londoners using underground stations to sleep in at night in 1940? Use Source B and your own knowledge to answer this question.

c How useful is Source C to an historian studying the effect of the Blitz on the civilian population? Use Source C and your own knowledge to answer this question.

d Is Source D an accurate interpretation of the state of civilian morale in Britain during the Blitz? Use Source D and your own knowledge to answer this question.

C SOURCE

A family of Londoners among the ruins of their Anderson shelter.

18 CIVILIAN MORALE

Key Issue

• Did civilian morale hold up during the Blitz?

The Blitz cost the *Luftwaffe* very few aircraft. In a raid by 200 aircraft the Germans would lose only three planes on average. German defences against the RAF were more effective and the British could expect to lose 15 planes for every 200 sent. However, the raids over Britain had no real effect on British aircraft production.

40,000 British civilians were killed and two million made homeless but it did not destroy the morale of the civilian population. Goebbels, Hitler's propaganda chief, decided that the British were showing such toughness because they were a 'Germanic race'.

President Roosevelt found it easier to persuade American opinion that now Britain was worth backing with vital military equipment and supplies. Strangely, the Blitz may have helped to improve morale since it did create a sense of community and shared danger which brought people closer together.

One lesson which the RAF's Bomber Command might have learned from the Blitz was that it was not easy to bomb a determined people into defeat. Air Chief Marshall Harris believed that RAF Bomber Command could do to the Germans what the *Luftwaffe* could not do to the British. He was wrong. But the bombing campaign over Germany did achieve other valuable results (see Chapter 10).

HOW DID PEOPLE COPE?

Though Britain's anti-aircraft defences didn't have much success against German bombers, other measures were taken to make it difficult for the enemy. All street and shop lights were turned off and homes had their windows blacked out with thick curtains or blinds. The black-out was supposed to make it more difficult for German bombers to find their targets at night. A city like London with all its lights on would be easily found otherwise.

TAKING SHELTER

By the time the war started, 38 million gas masks had already been issued. These were never needed since gas was not used in the Second World War – although people weren't to know this at the time. For a long time civilians carried their gas masks about with them in case of a gas attack. Even babies' prams were made gas-proof.

The real danger, though, came not from gas but bombs, and the government had already begun to prepare for air raids by issuing Anderson shelters as early as February 1939. Two million of these had been given to families in cities likely to be bombed by the time war broke out. They were free to families earning less than £250 a year. This was at a time when the average worker's wage was about £300 a year. Made from curved corrugated steel sheets bolted together, they were half buried in the garden (see photo, page 41). They were not very popular because they were damp and tended to flood. But most people preferred them to the communal brick shelters the government provided for the people in the local area.

What Londoners really wanted to use were the underground stations. At first the government would not allow them to be used as shelters. It was afraid that the people, once inside these deep shelters, wouldn't come out and this would be bad for morale. But in October 1940 the government had to give in and they were opened up.

The most popular stations were the deepest, such as Hampstead, and queues for these began as early as 10 a.m. In the deepest ones you couldn't hear the noise of the bombs and so had a better chance of getting some sleep. People were desperate for a place on the platform and fights occasionally took place.

After 10 p.m. the current was switched off and Londoners could sleep along the track. Those who couldn't get to the platform had to make do with a night on the stairs or escalators. At first there were no proper toilet facilities and the best that could be arranged were a few buckets screened off with a blanket.

'MEALS ON WHEELS'

In October 1940 a new Home Secretary, Herbert Morrison, was appointed. He immediately ordered deep shelters to be built for 70,000 people – though these weren't ready before the Blitz ended in May 1941. But 200,000 bunks and proper toilets were ready in the tube stations by Christmas 1940. Morrison also arranged for tube trains equipped with food and drink to pass each evening and early morning through those stations used as shelters.

'LAST ORDERS'?

The tube stations were used by only about 15 per cent of the London population. More than half preferred to sleep in their own homes where they used steel-framed Morrison shelters inside the house. These were about the same height as a table and big enough for a couple of adults and children to shelter beneath. Most of the rest used their Anderson shelters or the public shelters. Some, though, used no shelters at all and simply sat out the raids in pubs, singing very loudly so as not to hear the sound of the bombs. In some cases, no doubt, 'last orders' meant exactly that.

Those who lived in cities outside London had no tube stations in which to shelter. Many of these simply 'trekked' each night out into the country and slept where they could – barns, cowsheds, even ditches. There were 50,000 trekkers each night out of Plymouth. The government disapproved of trekking because it suggested that morale was cracking.

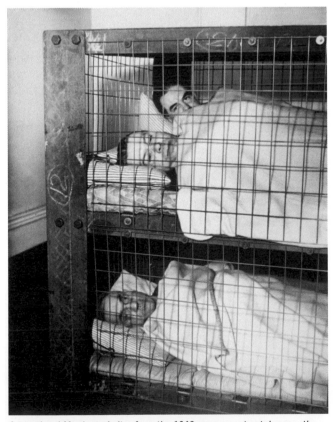

A two-tiered Morrison shelter from the 1942 government catalogue – the ultimate in comfort and luxury. They were free to poorer families and were used indoors.

CLEANING UP

The government had expected air raids and the devastation they would bring. What the government was not ready for were the large numbers of survivors. Help for those who had lost their homes was very badly organised at first. Eventually, compensation was paid for loss of homes and property. The houses of those who had left the cities were taken over and used to house the homeless.

Theft from bomb-damaged houses and shops (looting) could lead to the death penalty, but this drastic measure was never used. However, looting did go on. It was not unusual for rescue workers, firemen or demolition workers to help themselves to the odd possession left in a bombed-out house. It was seen, almost, as a reward for the gruesome and dangerous job they had.

Not all the bombs dropped by the Germans were supposed to explode when they hit the ground. Some, called parachute mines, came down slowly attached to parachutes, and exploded above or on the ground. These could cause more damage than the usual iron-cased bombs which sometimes buried themselves deep into the ground before exploding. This reduced the impact of the explosion.

Others were delayed-action bombs and were timed to explode hours and even days after they had hit the ground. These were very irritating and caused more disruption than ordinary impact bombs. This was because everyone within 600 metres of such a bomb had to be moved until it had been defused or went off.

None of the shelters protected you from a direct hit or from the blast of a near miss. Victims of blast often showed no signs of injury. The blast pressure simply crushed the internal organs of the body and sometimes stripped the clothes off them. Sometimes the blast would tear bodies apart. Recovering the pieces was not a pleasant job.

RESCUE WORK

Rescue work was a difficult job. Workers were paid about £3 a week – much less than the average wage at the time. Former building workers made the best rescue workers because they had a good knowledge of how the buildings had been made and where to look for survivors. The risk from collapsing buildings and broken water and gas pipes all made rescue work more difficult and dangerous. Some 5000 building workers had to be released from the army to help with the repairs to bomb-damaged homes.

Accommodation for those who lost their homes was very poor to begin with. For instance, 200–300 people crammed into a hall with only ten buckets for

Those bombed out of their homes urgently needed accommodation. Temporary homes like these were built for them, such as this one in Teddington, Middlesex.

toilets was not unusual. Eventually, the government provided temporary housing like the one shown above.

DID MORALE HOLD UP?

What the government feared most was defeatism among the population. Defeatism was the idea that the war couldn't be won and that Britain should agree peace terms with the Germans. **Mass Observation** reported very few examples of **defeatist** views but there was evidence of racial prejudice and a need to have someone innocent to blame. There were complaints, for example, against Jews for 'grabbing the best shelters' or 'not helping with the war effort'. One woman remembered her wartime schooldays and how a Jewish pupil was 'terribly, terribly victimised' and 'the terrible attitude that the Jews almost got what they deserved'.

Looting was another sign of morale under strain, as were the occasions when Churchill and the King and Queen were booed when they visited bombed streets in the East End. There was also bad feeling between the upper and lower classes. Plush West End hotels had their own private and comfortable shelters which the ordinary population couldn't use.

On one occasion this led to protesters occupying the shelter of the Savoy hotel.

This ill-feeling was made worse by the fact that most German bombs fell on the working class, industrial areas of big cities such as the East End of London. Few fell on the richer West End or comfortable suburbs. It seemed to some, therefore, that the poor were doing more than their fair share for the war.

Despite all this, morale did hold up and the civilian population remained firmly behind Churchill's policy of continuing the war until it was won. A different kind of spirit gradually emerged. As the historian, Peter Lewis, put it, 'Londoners as a whole did not lose their nerve, but they lost their reserve.'

A SOURCE

Harold Nicolson, a minister in the Ministry of Information, wrote this in his diary for 17 September, 1940:

Everybody is worried about the feeling in the East End, where there is much bitterness. It is said that even the King and Queen were booed the other day when they visited the destroyed areas. Clem [Attlee, the leader of the Labour Party] says there might be a revolution in this country.

B SOURCE

Government photograph designed to show the benefits of using communal brick-built shelters. One wall has been cut away to show the accommodation inside.

C SOURCE

This picture shows an anti-aircraft gun in action against German bombers. It was used as a wartime poster with the slogan 'Forward to Victory'.

D SOURCE

A modern historian on attitudes towards the rich in London during the Blitz (from *London at War*, Philip Ziegler, 1996).

There was still resentment of the rich to be found in the poorer quarters. The rich were known to be better protected; even if their houses did not enjoy deep concrete basements they could afford luxury shelters. Leslie Paul wrote indignantly of one that had cost £180 [£7000 in today's money] and boasted a lavatory and two bedrooms. They escaped to the country in their cars and refused to offer lifts to those who were trudging in the same direction.

Questions

a What does Source A tell you about how people reacted to the Blitz?
b Look at Source B. Why did the government produce this photograph in late 1940? Use Source B and your own knowledge to answer this question.
c How useful is Source C to an historian studying Britain during the Blitz? Use Source C and your own knowledge to answer this question.
d Is Source D an accurate interpretation of wartime spirit in England during the Blitz? Use Source D and your own knowledge to answer this question.

19 EVACUATION

Key Issue

What were the effects of evacuation?

Evacuation involved moving all of Britain's children from cities likely to be bombed to safer areas in the country. Plans already existed to evacuate Britain's children and they were quickly put into action in September 1939. 800,000 school children and 520,000 children under five (with their mothers) were soon sent by train to the country areas of Britain.

Evacuation was not compulsory and not all parents could bear to let their children go to stay with people they didn't know. This reluctance was understandable. But parents also knew that big cities were likely targets for German bombing. During the period of the 'phoney war' (September 1939–April 1940), there were no air raids. Gradually the parents arranged for their children to come back – only to go through it all again in September 1940 (and a third time during the V-bomb raids of 1944).

THE PROBLEMS

People with a spare room in country areas had to take in one or more children. The only choice they had was over which child they could take. Teachers went with their pupils too. They would all be crammed into the nearest available school and shared classrooms. When the evacuated children, or evacuees as they were called, arrived they were lined up for the host families to inspect. Clean looking girls were the most popular – they could help with domestic chores. Boys, though, were valued if they were big enough to help on the farm.

Sometimes brothers and sisters were split up, and dirty or unattractive children were left to last. All this proved to be a frightening experience for children a long way from their parents. Hosts were given an allowance of ten shillings (50p) a week – not much when a pair of stockings cost five shillings (25p). Some, nonetheless, tried to make money by providing very little for the children staying with them.

Some children didn't know how to use a toilet properly. In some inner city slums lacking proper toi-lets it was common practice to urinate on newspaper. Of course, their new, often middle-class hosts were horrified by such behaviour. The children often arrived with skin diseases and lice, and had never worn underwear, taken a bath or brushed their teeth. Bed-wetting, bad language and theft were other frequent complaints.

'I WEAR UNDERPANTS, DO YOU?'

For children like these from inner city slums, life in the country was another world. Green fields, orchards and farm animals were all new to them. One wrote to his mother, 'They call this spring, Mum, and they have one down here every year'. One delighted boy from the East End of London boasted to his friends: 'I wear underpants, do you?'

Many children loved the years they spent as evacuees as they enjoyed the benefits of country life: a healthy diet, fresh air and endless adventure. These children sometimes found it very difficult to get used to their old way of life when they returned to their homes after their evacuation.

Not all children, though, were sent to comfortable homes in delightful countryside. Some found themselves in much the same conditions they had left behind and others were worse off. Children's experiences of evacuation, therefore, were very different. But for all of them there was homesickness and the worry that their parents might be killed in an air raid. The government did provide cheap train tickets for parents to visit their children but only once a month.

CONSEQUENCES OF EVACUATION

The evacuation of so many children had very important social and political effects. Country families were often shocked by the health of the children they took in and the poverty they lived in when at home. It helped to convince people that a basic minimum standard of health and housing was a right for everyone. This was accepted during the war and the 1942 Beveridge Report promised changes. This set up what became known as the Welfare State in the years after the war.

In this sense, therefore, evacuation helped to bring about an important change in social attitudes. This in turn helped to bring about a new political belief that the state had a duty to provide much more in the way of basic standards of health and housing.

A SOURCE

A modern historian on the evacuation process in 1940 (from *The Forties*, Alan Jenkins, 1977).

In the country, kind people at first competed to be foster parents, choosing children as they arrived at local schools. There were constant difficulties about food: the East End of London seemed to live on fish and chips and wouldn't touch cabbage. There were children who had never seen an egg and thought you had to bite it like an apple. Some had never seen animals before and could not tell cows from sheep.

B SOURCE

Government poster, issued in 1940, concerning the evacuation of children.

C SOURCE

A government-approved photograph of children being evacuated by train.

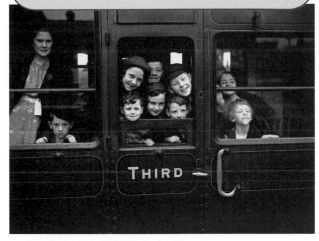

D SOURCE

A modern historian on the impact of evacuation (from *A People's War*, Peter Lewis, 1986).

Some believed that nothing but good could come out of the shock, as slum poverty was exposed at close quarters before the eyes of people more comfortably off.

Questions

a What does Source A tell you about the evacuation of children in 1940?

b Why were posters like Source B issued by the government in 1940? Use Source B and your own knowledge to answer this question.

c How useful is Source C to an historian studying evacuation during the war? Use Source C and your own knowledge to answer this question.

d Is Source D an accurate interpretation of the effects of evacuation on Britain during the Second World War? Use Source D and your own knowledge to answer this question.

20 FOOD SUPPLIES AND RATIONING

Rationing in the First World War started in the last year of the war. This time, the government was much quicker to ration food and essential supplies. On the whole, the population approved of rationing as a way to make sure everyone got a fair share of what was available at a reasonable price. Without rationing and price control, prices would have shot up beyond the ability of ordinary people to pay.

In November 1941 the government copied the points system used by the Germans. This system applied to food which was not rationed. This included fish, and tinned foods such as meat, fruit and puddings. Items which were in shortest supply cost the most points. For example, half a kilogram of tinned salmon would use up 32 points, but a tin of tomatoes would cost six points. Each month a person had 20 points to 'spend' on such goods. This limited the amount of unrationed goods rich people could buy and was, therefore, considered fairer.

Alternatives to the usual items were also found. Tea made from nettles was not popular but it had the edge over acorn coffee. Even less popular were dried eggs. Real eggs were very hard to come by. Egg powder, imported from the United States, was mixed with water and tasted like chalk. Another new food imported from the United States was 'Spam' (Supply Pressed American Meat). In 1944 the weekly cheese allowance per person dropped to under 60 grams – roughly a block of 4 centimetres by 7 centimetres.

People could not buy rationed goods where they wanted. They had to use the shopkeeper where they were registered. The amount of supplies a shopkeeper got depended on the number of customers registered with him. When customers bought goods he stamped the customers' ration cards and deducted the number of points used up. Sweets were also rationed. The monthly allowance was 250 grams of chocolate or its equivalent. But children's teeth were far healthier as a result.

BEATING THE SYSTEM

One way to save on food coupons was to eat out. The fact that the rich could eat fine meals in splendid hotels and get round the problem of rationing caused some anger in the working-class areas. The government decided that this was unfair. From 1942 restaurants (apart from the six plushest London hotels) were not allowed to charge more than five shillings (25p) for a meal – about three times the price of a packet of 20 cigarettes.

In 1943 the government set up 'British restaurants' which charged only one shilling (5p) for a very basic meal. This ready supply of cheap and nutritious food helped to make sure that the diet of the British population was much better during the war than it had ever been before.

Another way to get round rationing was to buy items on the black market. This was illegal but common, and items were expensive. Officials at the docks could be bribed to allow a few 'extra' items to be loaded onto a truck. These would then be delivered to the butcher's or greengrocer's shop. Shopkeepers would sell these from 'under the counter' to their best (and most trusted) customers. Customers went out of their way to be pleasant to their shopkeepers, especially butchers.

A more patriotic way to get round rationing was to grow your own food. The 'Dig for Victory' campaign encouraged people to grow their own vegetables in gardens and allotments. In 1939 there were 815,000 allotments but these had increased to 1.4 million in 1943.

UTILITY

In 1942 the government introduced the Utility symbol. Goods with this symbol were made cheaply but to a good standard. Clothing and furniture became Utility products and could be bought with coupons. These were sometimes half the price of non-utility items but the styles were very basic. Men's trousers were made without turn-ups. This was very unpopular. Women were encouraged to wear Utility suits (a one-piece trouser suit with a zip or buttons). These suits were especially recommended for use in shelters.

At least these suits meant that women didn't have to spend time hunting down pairs of stockings or painting their legs with gravy browning.

A SOURCE

A government leaflet offering advice on coping with textiles shortages.

B SOURCE

A government poster on dealing with food shortages.

C SOURCE

The impact of rationing (adapted from *An Underworld at War*, Donald Thomas, 2003).

The government showed that the wealthy and powerful were offered no favours if they broke the law. Despite this, the feeling persisted that the rich did not share the hardships suffered by the less well-off.

D SOURCE

An American journalist, Mollie Panter-Downes, describes the impact of rationing for her American readers in August 1941 (from *Hearts Undefeated*, ed. Jenny Hartley, 1994).

On the whole, the food situation, although it is far from good, is a long way from being desperate. The average number of calories which each member of the population consumed during the first year of the war was only one per cent lower than it was in peacetime and it is expected that it will be no lower this year. The urban poor come off the worst, because of their dislike for vegetables and cereals. The rural poor do a good deal better because they grow a lot of vegetables and generally keep a few chickens.

Questions

a What does Source D tell you about rationing in 1941?

b Why was Source B distributed in Britain during the war? Use Source B and your own knowledge to answer this question.

c How useful is Source A to an historian studying rationing? Use Source A and your own knowledge to answer this question.

d Is Source C an accurate interpretation of how rationing was viewed by the public? Use Source C and your own knowledge to answer this question.

'THIS WAR IS EVERYBODY'S'

In November 1939 the editor of the magazine *Mother and Home* wrote: 'The last was a soldier's war. This one is everybody's.' The purpose of this and the next two chapters is to decide just how much the war did change things for women.

Certainly, the statistics suggest that a lot did change. By September 1943 there were nearly eight million women in paid work. This is three million more than when the war started. There were another one million women in the Women's Voluntary Services. The munitions industries saw a big increase in women workers – up from 500,000 to two million. From December 1941 women between the ages of 20 and 30 could be **conscripted** into the women's armed forces – though not for combat duty.

In the same year, women between 18 and 40 could be made to work in war industries. In 1943 the government widened these age limits so more women could be used. By then nine out of every ten single women were doing some kind of war work.

'NICE GIRLS DON'T'

After 1941 the government could tell single women to go to any part of the country and to work in whatever industry it decided. It could also order them to join one of the women's armed services (see Chapter 22). The government had asked women to volunteer for a variety of war industries but the response hadn't been good. Women were afraid that they would be sent away from home and forced to stay with strangers (called 'being **billeted**'). Factory work with its 12-hour shifts was not appealing to women, and fathers and boyfriends tended to object to them working as well. There still remained an attitude that 'nice girls' didn't work in factories.

DILUTION

The government, at first, didn't conscript married women, and women with children under 14 could not be sent to work away from home. But from 1943 the government began finding work for married women as well. It must be said that the attitudes of male workers, in some cases, were not welcoming. They were afraid that unskilled women would start doing skilled, male workers' jobs and for less money. This was known as dilution. Dilution, they argued, would force down wages and cost skilled workers their jobs.

These men's fears were increased when women were promised equal pay for doing the same job as men. However, this was easily got round. The job done by women – even if identical to that done by men – was simply renamed and paid a lower rate. The government didn't help the cause of women's equality, either. It refused to pay its women civilian and military employees the same rate as men. The difference in rates of pay angered most women. In some cases, they weren't even paid the men's unskilled rate for the skilled work they were doing.

The government failed in other areas, too. Only one child in four under the age of five was in a public nursery. The mothers of the other children had to make their own arrangements for child care while they worked. Even when concessions were made, there was a sting in the tail. A 12-hour shift meant that the shops were closed when the women finished work. The only thing they could do, therefore, was to miss work if they needed to go shopping.

This explains why absenteeism among women was twice the rate it was for men. Women working a full week of 57–60 hours were given 'shopping time' to allow them to get essential shopping done in working hours. Shopping for supplies in wartime Britain was a difficult task and many women must have felt their working day never ended.

Despite all this, many women were pleased to be involved in useful work which helped the war effort. Even if they weren't as well paid as the men, they were still earning much more than they were used to getting before the war. Before the war women earned in the region of £2 a week and men about £3. During the war some women doing dangerous munitions work were earning £10 a week and £5 was common in the aircraft industry.

A SOURCE

Kay Ekevall represented women workers in the shipbuilding firm, Redpath Brown (from *Don't You Know There's a War On?*, J Croall, 1989).

Women took part in most of the jobs, such as crane-driving, painting, welding. I became a welder when there were both men and women trainees, but the men were paid more than the women. We had several battles over equal pay after we were used on the same jobs as the men . . . By the end of my time we had managed to get close to the men's wage.

B SOURCE

A government poster encouraging women to work for the war effort.

JUST A GOOD AFTERNOON'S WORK

C SOURCE

A comment by one woman to **Mass Observation** in 1942.

I do feel that equal pay would upset the relations between the sexes. Personally, I like a man to have more money than me. It gives me twice as much pleasure to have a dress bought for me by a kindly man than to buy it myself, and this is because I am feminine.

D SOURCE

A modern historian on the impact of the war on women (from *Life on the Home Front*, Tim Healey, 1993).

Many women enjoyed their transformed lives, with the chance to earn wages, and the new challenges, and new freedoms.

Questions

a What does Source A tell us about the role played by women in the war?
b Why did the government issue posters like Source B during the war? Use Source B and your own knowledge to answer the question.
c How useful is Source C to an historian studying the attitudes of women during the war? Use Source C and your own knowledge to answer the question.
d Is Source D an accurate interpretation of how the war affected women? Use Source D and your own knowledge to answer the question.

Make brief notes under the following headings:
• Conscription of women
• Dilution
• Women's pay
• Absenteeism

When women were **conscripted** in 1941 they were, in theory, given the choice of joining one of the armed forces or working in the factories. They could join either the Women's Royal Naval Service known as Wrens (WRNS), the Women's Auxiliary Air Force (WAAF), or the Auxiliary Territorial Service (ATS).

The WRNS was the most popular service, followed by the WAAF. For one thing women thought their blue uniforms were more attractive and feminine than the dull khaki of the ATS. The writer of one letter to *The Times* in 1941 complained that: 'Khaki is a colour detested by every woman and makes a well-developed girl look vulgar.'

In practice, women who were conscripted had no choice as to which of the services they joined. The WRNS and WAAF already had waiting lists so all the new conscripts had to join the ATS. In 1944 there were 450,000 women in these three services with 212,000 of them in the ATS. This allowed many men to do combat duty and this was an important part of women's contribution to the war effort.

Women in the WRNS and the WAAF were generally thought to be more respectable, while those in the army's ATS had a 'reputation' for loose behaviour. Such ideas about women in uniform did not make it easy for women to join and many were not keen. Some women so hated the ATS that they deliberately got pregnant to get themselves dismissed from the army. Public opinion could be very hurtful, and husbands and fathers were even more against their womenfolk joining one of the armed forces than they were against them working.

The general belief was that single women in the armed services were more likely to get pregnant than single women in civilian jobs. Government statistics proved the opposite was true but the old attitudes lived on.

'TOILETS WITH DOORS, PLEASE!'

Women's fears about life in the armed services were probably made worse by finding out that the lavatories had no doors on them. This was common practice for the men and nobody had given much thought to the idea that women would be unhappy with the arrangement.

Women soon found themselves doing tough and dangerous jobs. They worked as mechanics, welders, pilots, carpenters and gunners on anti-aircraft guns – though they weren't allowed to fire the guns. They also operated the searchlights for the anti-aircraft guns. The ATS was certainly the most dangerous of the services open to women. 335 were killed and another 300 wounded. Women also served as ferry pilots, flying the newly built planes to their air bases.

DOUBLE STANDARDS

But it should be remembered that traditional, sexist attitudes did not suddenly disappear. The vast majority of women in these services worked as cleaners, cooks and secretaries. Women ferry pilots flew planes without radios because RAF chiefs feared they would use them to gossip to each other! This type of flying, called instrument-flying, was more difficult.

The decision in 1941 to have mixed anti-aircraft gun units was a controversial one. Not even the fact that Churchill's daughter worked on one helped to get rid of ugly rumours about the women in these units (Source A). There were about 50,000 women in the ATS who helped to operate anti-aircraft guns. The fact that they had to share accommodation with the men and lived close to each other led to heavy criticism.

Women in the armed services had to operate under double standards. They were expected to do skilled, tough and sometimes dangerous jobs and yet still be feminine. This created extra strains for women which the men didn't have, as ferry pilot Diana Barnato Walker points out:

'I always thought, if I crashed, I'd rather be killed than disabled. A damaged woman has nothing. Men can function without a leg or arm, or burnt, and they are considered heroes. People accept them. But a damaged woman? I think it was my greatest fear.'

A SOURCE

Joan Savage Cowey worked in a mixed anti-aircraft gun crew (from *Women in War*, Shelley Saywell, 1985).

There was a feeling that we were sort of loose women living in tents with men. They called us 'officers' groundsheets' – we got that all the time. They thought we were there to entertain the troops. The American soldiers were worse. They'd say the Brits had it really good, having us girls along to keep them happy. The whole thing – all the criticism of us – just had to do with sex.

B SOURCE

Recruitment poster for the ATS and WAAF, issued in 1943.

THOUSANDS OF WOMEN NEEDED NOW IN THE ATS, WAAF

VITAL TO THE OFFENSIVE

NO BRITISH WOMAN WILL STAND ASIDE AS THE HUN APPROACHES

WHERE TO VOLUNTEER

Full information at the nearest recruiting centre or your employment exchange

D SOURCE

A modern history book on the impact of the war on British women (adapted from *The Oxford Companion to the Second World War*, ed. I Dear, 1995).

In the UK, the recruitment of women into the armed forces was held back by persistent rumours of immorality among servicewomen.

Questions

a What does Source A tell us about attitudes to women in the armed forces?

b Why did the government issue posters like Source B? Use Source B and your own knowledge to answer this question.

c How useful is Source C to an historian studying the role of women in the armed forces? Use Source C and your own knowledge to answer this question.

d Is Source D an accurate interpretation of the problems faced by women in the armed forces during the war? Use Source D and your own knowledge to answer this question.

C SOURCE

A painting by Dame Laura Knight of women in the WAAF in Coventry learning to operate a barrage balloon.

WOMEN'S LAND ARMY

Attitudes to women working in farming saw dramatic changes. There was a desperate need for farm labour from the start of the war. Before September 1939 there had been 550,000 men working on the land and 55,000 women. The number of men dropped and 80,000 women joined the Women's Land Army (WLA) to make up the difference.

Farmers doubted that women could do the physically demanding and dirty work needed on Britain's farms. The idea that women could drive tractors, plough, cut down trees and shear sheep seemed daft. What made it more unlikely was that a third of the women came from the towns and were not used to country life at all. Women in the WLA had no choice where they worked. They were **billeted** in remote areas in very basic conditions.

Many spoke of having to travel to the public baths for a proper wash.

WLA pay was poor. In 1944 they earned £2.40 a week – less than the female average wage of £3 – and half of that went on lodgings. Despite this, the Land Girls were a success. They proved themselves more than able to cope with the tough jobs and handled farm animals particularly well. Like women in the armed services, they had to put up with the same sexist comments about their supposed 'lack of moral standards'.

WHAT DID THE WAR CHANGE?

Clearly the many varied, difficult and skilled jobs women did during the war proved that women could do nearly every job that men could do. Though they weren't expected to carry the same weights as men, they did the same jobs.

However, there is plenty of evidence to suggest that women never got away from their traditional role as far as people's thinking went. Men were not enthusiastic supporters of this new, independent role for women – and neither were all women. By June

1943 there were nearly eight million women in paid work but this had dropped to six million by June 1947.

This fall was not because the government tried hard to get women out of their wartime jobs to make room for men. There was a labour shortage after the war and the government was keen for women to stay in their jobs. They left their jobs because they wanted to return to the home. Government surveys in 1943 and again in 1947 revealed that 58 per cent of women believed that married women should not go out to work.

Hopes that women had carved out a new role for themselves as a result of the war soon faded. This advert from the 1950s still promotes the assumption that a woman's proper role was 'homemaking'.

Many had delayed having children during the war and now they decided to start their families. However, some of these married women went on to find jobs in the 1950s.

Women's career opportunities weren't drastically improved by the war, either. Women during the war found many jobs in new areas of employment such as metal manufacturing and engineering. But these opportunities only lasted as long as the war. The shutting down of nurseries after the war meant the end of jobs for women with children. They continued to make only slow progress in professions like medicine and law. By 1961 only 15 per cent of doctors and a mere 3.5 per cent of lawyers were women.

EQUAL PAY?

After growing protests by women, the government agreed in 1944 to set up a Royal Commission to investigate the issue of equal pay for women. Conveniently, it didn't report until a year after the war in 1946. The average male manual worker's wage in 1943 was £5.70 a week while the wage for a woman was £3. The Commission accepted this was true but reported that it was a difficult matter because women often did different jobs from men and so equal pay wasn't an issue.

A SOURCE

Mona Marshall worked in the steel industry during the war (from *A People's War*, Peter Lewis, 1986).

To be quite honest, the war was the best thing that ever happened to us. I was as green as grass and terrified if anyone spoke to me. I had been brought up not to argue. My generation of women had been taught to do as we were told. At work you did exactly as your boss told you and you went home to do exactly as your husband told you. The war changed all that. The war made me stand on my own two feet.

B SOURCE

A photograph of three women in the Women's Land Army, May 1942.

What could not be taken away from women was the new self-respect that the war had given them. There is no doubt that they were much more confident about themselves and their abilities. Many enjoyed the independence and freedom the war had given them. If these changes had come too late for these women, then their daughters would benefit in the late 1960s when the feminist movement began its campaign for women's rights.

C SOURCE

Percentage of women in paid work:

	Single women	Married women	All women
1911	69	10	35
1921	68	9	34
1931	72	10	34
1951	73	22	35

D SOURCE

The historian, Carol Harris, on the impact of the war on women (from the BBC History website).

It was understood throughout the war that what Britain's women were doing was really 'a man's job'. So many of them were dismissed from their work once peace was declared.

Questions

a **What does Source A suggest about how the war affected women?**

b **Why was the government keen to show Source B as an image of the Women's Land Army?**

c **How useful is Source C to an historian studying how the position of women changed as a result of the Second World War? Use Source C and your own knowledge to answer this question.**

d **Is Source D an accurate interpretation of how the war affected the position of women in society? Use Source D and your own knowledge to answer this question.**

Make brief notes under the following headings:
- Women's Land Army
- Women's employment
- Career opportunities
- Equal pay

Key Issue

- How did the war change life in Britain?

The war changed Britain a great deal and this became very obvious to Churchill as early as July 1945. He lost Britain's first general election for ten years. The reasons for Churchill's defeat sum up many of the changes which had taken place in six years of war.

Winston Churchill had been an inspiring leader of Britain. He became Prime Minister at a time when Britain seemed about to be invaded. After the defeat of France in June 1940, Britain faced the might of Hitler's military power alone. Defeat seemed likely. It was at this time that Churchill made his greatest contribution to Britain's eventual victory – by keeping up the people's morale when all seemed lost. But, once the war against Germany was won, the British public turned their back on Churchill and voted him out of office.

THE BEVERIDGE REPORT, 1942

In December 1942 Sir William Beveridge presented his report on Britain's social services. He proposed that after the war *all* citizens should be entitled to certain *free* benefits. Most of these benefits, such as unemployment and sickness benefits, existed already but they were not easy to get. Before the war, medical treatment had to be paid for and how to pay doctor's bills was a constant worry for the poor. Beveridge proposed allowances of five shillings (about £10 in today's value) for all children after the first in each family and a National Health Service which would provide free medical care. These benefits would be paid for by taxing each person's earnings. The benefits only provided a minimum standard of living or care but the Report was tremendously popular.

Churchill, though, wasn't keen on the proposals and his lack of interest in them was quickly noticed. The Labour Party, on the other hand, was fully in support of the Beveridge Report. In 1945 voters made it clear which party they trusted to carry out Beveridge's proposals. The voters didn't trust Churchill and his Conservative Party.

THE ELECTION CAMPAIGN

Churchill also made some mistakes in the 1945 election campaign. He concentrated on international issues and not domestic ones to do with Britain. Churchill told the voters that **communist** Russia and its leader, Stalin, were the new threat to Britain. But the people didn't share his worries about communism. They wanted to know about what ideas Churchill had for making Britain a better place to live in.

Churchill had little to say on the things that mattered to the people. They wanted to know how the bombed-out houses would be replaced and what medical treatment they could get under the National Health Service (NHS). Instead of this, Churchill told them that if Labour won the election, they would set up a British version of the Gestapo to keep control. The Gestapo was Hitler's vicious secret police, responsible for arresting and terrorising opponents. This was a terrible insult to the Labour Party. Labour

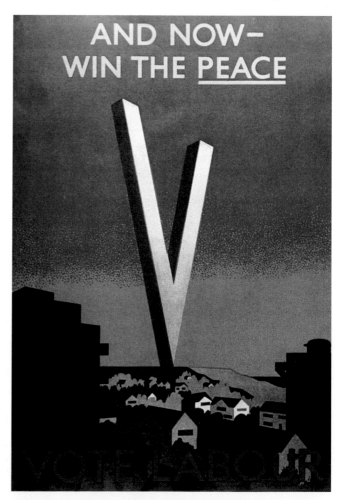

This 1945 Labour election poster echoed what the British public felt. There would have to be a new Britain, different from, and better than, the one before the war, to make the country's sacrifices worthwhile.

had not only supported the government in the war against the Nazis but had also been part of the **coalition government** set up by Churchill.

LABOUR: 'FACING THE FUTURE'

Churchill had clearly lost touch with the people. Clement Attlee, the Labour leader, on the other hand, was in touch with the public mood. During the election campaign he wisely concentrated on plans for the future of Britain. The Labour policy was called 'Let Us Face the Future'. It spelt out how Labour would carry out Beveridge's proposals and nationalise key industries like coal, electricity, and the railways. It promised to build four million council homes for those who couldn't afford to buy their own.

Labour won a crushing victory. Apart from the 1997 election, it was the biggest in its history.

Labour won 393 out of 640 seats and the Conservatives only 213.

THE KHAKI VOTE

The British people were not prepared to go back to the same Britain which existed before the war. That is what had happened after the First World War. This time things would be different, they decided. It took three weeks for the result of the election in July 1945 to become known. This was because of the 'khaki vote'. These were votes of those men and women serving in the armed forces across the world – especially in the Far East where Japan was still fighting. They voted in large numbers for Labour. There was considerable ill-feeling between the officers and the lower ranks in the forces, as you can see from Source C.

Vicky, the cartoonist who drew this cartoon in June 1944, was clearly worried about what Britain would be like after the war. The end of the Great War brought only unemployment for its returning soldiers. Would this happen again?

1945: ALL CHANGE?

The British people were rightly proud of the part they had played in defeating Nazi Germany and then Japan. They felt that it proved that the British way of doing things was still best and that Britain was still a great world power. They also felt that the victory now provided an opportunity to rebuild a different and better Britain.

POWER TO THE PEOPLE

In some ways, Britain did change. The historian, Arthur Marwick, believes that the war brought about an important change in attitudes. During the war most people came to believe that the government should have a much greater role in running the economy and greater influence over people's lives. This, after all, was how the war had been won. This is exactly what Labour had always believed and explains why the party won the 1945 election so easily. The Labour government's **nationalisation** policies from 1946–9 reflected this belief.

Britain did change and not just because of new ideas about economic policy. Working-class people, Marwick claims, were no longer prepared to put up with the old pre-war attitudes about class. Many before the war had accepted that rich people, the upper class, were the right people to run the country. But the war gave ordinary people the confidence to take on the job themselves. That's why they voted the Labour Party into power in 1945.

People came to believe that poverty, slum housing, unemployment, bad diet and poor health could be got rid of. In short, the war led people to expect more from life. They were not going to be fobbed off as they had been after the First World War. The people demanded a 'welfare state' which would provide all these benefits for free.

BRITAIN IN DEBT

Some historians, like Corelli Barnett, have argued that Britain could not afford to provide these improvements after the war and shouldn't have tried. The war had left Britain owing a huge sum of money. More had to be borrowed from the USA for Britain to pay its bills. Barnett suggests that the money spent on the Welfare State should have been spent on new, up-to-date machinery and equipment for Britain's industries. Only later, when Britain could afford it, should money have been spent on the welfare benefits.

Some **socialist** historians have written that the Labour government of 1945–51 didn't do that much to change British society. The Labour Party's policies between 1945–51, they claim, weren't very socialist at all. Most of what Clement Attlee's Labour government did in these years had already been agreed by the wartime coalition government – a government which included Conservatives. What Labour did was to make **capitalism** work more efficiently and more fairly, but they didn't really change the system.

THE END OF GLORY?

The fact that Labour wasn't really very socialist would have been little consolation to Conservatives like Churchill. They had three basic policies for Britain. They wanted to keep Britain as a powerful and independent state, with an important role in world affairs. They wanted to defend the British Empire, and they wanted to keep Britain Conservative and Labour out of power.

All these hopes quickly fell apart. Labour won its second biggest election victory ever in 1945. After the war, Britain became very much the junior partner in the relationship between Britain and the United States. Britain gradually lost its role as a major world power. For people like Churchill the worst thing was that by the early 1960s almost all of the British Empire had gone, as each of Britain's colonies became independent.

Churchill lived until 1965 and saw all this happen. A grateful British public recognised its debt to the wartime leader. Churchill was given a State funeral – an honour usually reserved only for kings and queens. Victory in the war and the 1945 election should have been Churchill's most glorious moment. Twenty years later 1945 must have seemed more like the end of glory, than its beginning.

A SOURCE

One person's view of the war (from *Now the War is Over*, P Addison, 1985).

People were more together. They met in air raid shelters, in the tubes at night, they were in the Home Guard, or they queued for Spam or whatever . . . Everybody really lost a lot of their shyness about talking to their next door neighbours . . . and this was the spirit that I think a lot of people hoped would continue after the war.

B SOURCE

This poster was issued by the education section of the British army in 1944. The building shown is a new health centre opened in Finsbury, north London. The government disapproved of the poster and ordered it to be withdrawn.

C SOURCE

Frank Mayes, a British communist, remembers the reaction of British sailors to the news of Labour's victory (from *Don't You Know There's a War On?*, J Croall, 1989).

A great cheer went up and one of the officers said, 'Well, that's it. I'm not going back to England.' A sailor said to him, 'Well, we won't bloody miss you.' It was the only time I heard of a seaman speak to an officer like that. We all thought that a fairer, new Britain was going to come about. Of course it didn't, and we were very soon disappointed.

D SOURCE

John Beavan, editor of the Labour-supporting *Daily Herald* newspaper, on Britain during the war (from *A People's War*, Peter Lewis, 1986).

There was this general feeling that we were one nation – a feeling of equality, that everybody was valuable, that everybody's effort counted. It was a much more equal society than we had before.

Questions

a What does Source A tell us about how people remembered the war?
b Why was this poster issued in 1944? Use Source B and your own knowledge to answer this question.
c How useful is Source C to an historian studying attitudes among the British people in 1945? Use Source C and your own knowledge to answer this question.
d Is Source D an accurate interpretation of how Britain was during the war? Use Source D and your own knowledge to answer this question.

Make brief notes under the following headings:
- The Beveridge Report
- 1945 election campaign
- Labour's policies
- The khaki vote
- Impact of the war on Britain

The use of the correct *technique* is the key to success in source evaluation papers and this counts for much more than the application of knowledge. The best way to improve this technique, as for any skill, is practice.

EDEXCEL

The sources on which these examples are based are on p 3.

(a) *What can you learn from Source A about Churchill's views on the Munich Agreement? (4 marks)*

TECHNIQUE

- To get more than 2 for this question you must read between the lines and make an inference i.e. write something that the source *suggests* or *implies*.
- A couple of inferences with some explanation will be enough for 4 marks.
- It is a good idea to start your answer with the same phrase each time i.e 'Source A suggests. . .' or 'Source A implies . . .'
- Example: *'Source A implies that the British government had only postponed the inevitable conflict with Germany ('do not suppose that this is the end') and when that conflict did come, Britain would be worse off than it was in 1938. He also suggests that Britain was now at the mercy of Hitler who could choose his time when to attack.'*

(b) *Does Source C support the evidence of Sources A and B about the Munich Agreement? (6 marks)*

TECHNIQUE

- It is essential (for 5/6 marks) to discuss the extent to which the sources agree.
- Do this in a concluding sentence or sentences.
- Do not compare Source A with B. You will get no credit for this.
- Do not comment on whether the sources are reliable or who wrote them. You will get no credit for this.
- Compare Source C with A then C with B. Do not compare C with A and B together.
- Example: *'Source C states that Britain had failed to re-arm and this is supported by Source A where Churchill says the government did not 're-arm ourselves in time'. Source B, however, contradicts C because it claims that 'we re-armed during this year'. On the other hand, C does describe appeasement as a 'cowardly' policy and this is implied in B when it refers to Britain losing its 'good name' because of Munich.*
  On balance, Source C is partly supported by A and B but both of these refer to issues not discussed in C, such as the loss of the Czech military.'
- Note the use of appropriate connectives: 'However', On the other hand', 'On balance'.

(c) *How useful are Sources D and E as evidence of the success or failure of the policy of appeasement? (8 marks)*

TECHNIQUE

- It is essential in this question to write about the *type*, **provenance** or *purpose* of the sources if you are to get more than 6 marks i.e. achieve a Level 3 response.
- You don't have to comment on all three to get to Level 3.
- All of the sources in this question will be useful for something.
- A source is still useful, even if it isn't reliable.
- Example: *'Source E is very useful in explaining the success of appeasement. It shows how British air-power increased dramatically in the year after Munich and that Britain had nearly caught up with Germany. This helps to prove that Munich 'bought' Britain a valuable year to re-arm. Furthermore, though we have not been told exactly where the statistics come from, there is no reason to doubt their accuracy and they have been quoted in a recent history book.'*

(d) *'Chamberlain's policy of appeasement towards Germany was the right policy at the time.' Use the sources and your own knowledge to explain whether you agree with this view. (12 marks)*

TECHNIQUE

- It is not a good idea to go through the sources one by one, from A to F.
- Group the sources into those which support the point of view of the question and those which do not. Then discuss them.
- You don't have to comment on all the sources to get high marks but three is a minimum.
- You must use both the sources and your own knowledge; otherwise you will lose half the marks available.
- You must finish with a conclusion which makes clear what your judgement of the question is. There isn't a right or wrong answer to this question – you just need to support it with appropriate use of the evidence.

- Example: *'In conclusion, the sources are divided on whether appeasement was the right policy. Sources A and B are very critical, and C is also opposed. On the other hand, there is plenty of evidence in favour in Sources D, E, and F but D and E are primary sources which simply reflect the public's relief at the time. In hindsight, the outbreak of war in 1939 must be seen as evidence of the failure of appeasement.'*

AQA

The sources on which these examples are based are on pp10–11.

(a) *What does Source A tell us about the evacuation from Dunkirk? (3 marks)*

TECHNIQUE

- This is a straightforward question and you need only provide three short sentences, each containing a relevant piece of information from the source or make an inference – i.e. write something that the source *suggests* or *implies*.
- You will get no credit for adding knowledge of your own.
- Do not waste time by writing too much here.
- Example: *'Source A tells us that the men evacuated from Dunkirk were in good spirits, joking and even playing football. They were very keen to get back into battle.'*
- Or you could make an inference: *'Source A suggests that the newspapers at the time tried hard to give a positive image of the evacuation so as to keep up morale with stories of troops eager to get back at the Germans, despite their terrible experience of having their ship sunk.'*

(b) *Why were photographs like Source B officially approved at the time? Use Source B and your own knowledge to answer the question. (6 marks)*

TECHNIQUE

- You must use both the source and some own knowledge to get more than two marks.
- You must also provide more than one reason for marks in the higher levels.
- Comment on the purpose of the source and its historical context.
- Example: *'The government approved photographs like this because it helped to keep up public morale at a time when the military situation was really bad. The BEF had just been driven out of France with the loss of huge amounts of valuable military equipment and France was about to surrender. A photograph of smiling British troops would help to cover up the seriousness of this defeat. The photograph was intended as propaganda and it did its job. Even today, people still talk of the 'miracle' of Dunkirk rather than the defeat of Dunkirk.'*

(c) *How useful is Source C to an historian studying the evacuation from Dunkirk? Use Source C and your own knowledge to answer this question. (8 marks)*

TECHNIQUE

- You need to make use of the provenance of the source to score top marks and discuss its purpose.
- You should also test its usefulness by comparing it with your own knowledge.
- Don't confuse usefulness with reliability – a source is still useful even if it isn't reliable.
- Example: *'We have good details of the provenance of this source. We know the artist's name and the fact that he was an official war artist at the time. A key element of the Dunkirk 'myth' is the part played by over 900 'little' ships which set out to bring back over 330,000 troops. These are clearly shown here. An historian would use this painting as evidence of how the myth was created at the time. The painting is also accurate in that ships of the type painted here did take part in the evacuation and this would add to its usefulness. Wilkinson was an official war artist and this painting has a propaganda role. An historian would get a good understanding of how the government wanted the evacuation to be shown to the public.'*

(d) *Is Source D an accurate interpretation of the evacuation? Use Source D and your own knowledge to answer this question. (8 marks)*

TECHNIQUE

- Once again, it is important to discuss the provenance of the source and to provide detailed own knowledge to help decide how fair or accurate the interpretation is.
- You must also consider the type of source it is and its content.
- Ask yourself whether the content is typical of what you already know about the event. If it is, then it is more likely to be accurate.
- Example: *'The writers, modern historians, clearly see the evacuation as a "fantastic success". The book was written in 1999 so there is no need for them to maintain war-time morale but they see the evacuation of 'over a third of a million men' as a great achievement, which it was. In addition, it mentions the capture of the French rearguard. In this sense it is accurate.*
  On the other hand, there is no mention of the vast stocks of equipment left behind or the fact that the BEF had failed to defend France against the Germans. These are not examples of a "fantastic success". In this sense, the interpretation is not accurate because it leaves out key evidence.'
- Note the use of appropriate connectives: 'On the other hand', 'In addition'.

GLOSSARY

air-raid warden – an individual whose job was to help the public during air-raids and make sure that air-raid precautions (ARP) were followed

Allies – those countries at war with the Axis i.e. Britain, the USA and the Soviet Union

appeasement – a policy of making concessions to avoid conflict; the policy followed by Britain and France towards Germany between 1935–39

armaments – weapons of war

Axis – the defeated powers in the war: Germany, Italy and Japan; named after the Rome–Berlin–Tokyo Axis agreement which linked them together

billeting – forcing householders with spare rooms to take in families escaping from the bombing or workers involved in the war effort

Blitzkrieg – a new type of warfare first used by the Germans which achieved the key elements of surprise and speed by using aircraft, tanks and troops transported by trucks

capitalism – an economic system in which the government's role is very limited and businesses are owned privately

censorship – the policy of preventing people from getting information the government wants to keep secret

coalition government – a government made up of two or more political parties working together

communist – someone who believes in a system of government that opposes individual freedom and democracy and favours government control of all major industries

conscription – forcing men, and sometimes women, to enlist in the armed forces

convoy – a group of merchant ships escorted by destroyers for protection against U-boats

defeatist – someone who thinks his country will lose the war and lowers morale by saying so

dictator – a ruler who has total control over a country and allows no opposition

fascist – someone against democracy and individual freedoms

Fifth Columnist – an enemy spy or supporter of the enemy

Great Depression – the period in the 1930s when there was high unemployment and much hardship

internment – the policy of arresting enemy citizens (i.e. Germans and Italians in the Second World War who lived in Britain) and sending them to camps

Lebensraum – the German for 'living space' and Hitler's policy of conquest in the east of Europe

Mass Observation – an organisation whose members reported to the government conversations and interviews with members of the public

merchant ship – unarmed ship used for carrying supplies

nationalisation – the policy of the government or state taking over one or more privately owned industries

Nazism – a system of government which opposes individual freedom, democracy and favours extreme nationalism and ideas of racial superiority

partisan – a civilian fighter against enemy forces occupying his or her country; also called a resistance fighter. Soldiers, separated from their units, also joined the partisans

provenance – where a source comes from – who wrote it? When? Who was intended to read it? What role did the writer have? Knowing about a source's provenance is important for deciding its value and reliability

Quisling – Vidkun Quisling, a Norwegian, formed a pro-Nazi government in Norway under German control. In 1945 he was executed as a traitor. 'Quisling' has since become a word for traitor or collaborator

raw materials – materials such as coal, iron and oil which are used to manufacture other products

reconnaissance – getting information about the enemy, usually by aircraft

reprisal – the arrest and often execution of hostages in revenge for an attack by resistance groups

resistance – organised groups of civilians who fought against the Nazis occupying their country

SS (Schutz Staffeln) – German for protection squads; the SS ran Hitler's concentration camps and committed the worst crimes of the war

Second Front – the invasion of German-occupied France, which finally took place in June 1944 (Russia was the 'first' front)

socialist – someone who believes the government should run the country in the interests of the working people and not the rich

unconditional surrender – when a country surrenders unconditionally it has to accept all the terms imposed by the winners

Vichy France – that part of southern France which the Germans did not occupy. Instead, they allowed a pro-German French government to operate there from the town of Vichy until November 1942

ACKNOWLEDGEMENTS

The publishers would like to thank the following individuals, institutions and companies for permission to reproduce copyright illustrations in this book:
The Advertising Archive Ltd: p. 54; AKG Images: p. 28; © Bettmann/CORBIS: pp 21 (top), 23; © Corbis: p. 33; John Frost Newspaper Library: pp 15, 35 (bottom); The Hoover Institution: pp 19 (top), 26; Hulton Archive/Getty Images: pp 3, 4 (top), 7, 10, 13, 21 (bottom), 35 (top), 36, 41 (top and bottom), 43, 44, 55; © Hulton-Deutsch Collection/CORBIS: pp 4 (bottom), 12, 45 (top), 47 (top); with the permission of the Trustees of the Imperial War Museum, London: pp 11 'Little Ships at Dunkirk' by Norman Wilkinson (The Art Archive/© IWM), 17 (IWM UK1962), 19 (bottom) (IWM RUS 1263), 31 (top) (IWM PST 0658), 38 (IWM MH 6718), 47 (bottom) (IWM PST 3095), 49 (IWM 2892), 53 (bottom) 'A Balloon Site, Coventry' by Dame Laura Knight (IWM LD 2750), 59; David Low/*Evening Standard*/Centre for the Study of Cartoons and Caricature, University of Kent at Canterbury © Atlantic Syndication: p. 9; The National Archives: pp 45 (bottom) (INF 3/1707), 49 (top) (INF 13/144 (18)); The National Archives/HIP/Topham Picturepoint: pp 22, 53 (top); The National Archives, USA: p 31 (bottom) (111-C-5904); Peter Newark's Pictures: p. 37; Office of War Information, Washington DC: p. 27; © Popperfoto.com: p. 39; Public Record Office p. 51 (INF 3/400); © Topham Picturepoint: pp 25, 56; Vicky/News Chronicle/Centre for the Study of Cartoons and Caricature, University of Kent at Canterbury, © Atlantic Syndication: p. 57.

The publishers would also like to thank the following for permission to reproduce material in this book:
Allen Lane for the extracts from *Russia's War* by R Overy (1997); Allen & Unwin for the extracts from *The Ministry of Morale* by I McClaine (1979); Aurum Press Ltd for the extracts from *The World War II Databook* by J Ellis (1993); the BBC for the extract from the BBC history website; BBC Books for the extract from *The Battle of the Atlantic* by A Williams (2002); David Higham Associates for the extract from *Now the War is Over* by P Addison (BBC/Jonathan Cape, 1985); Bloomsbury Publishing for the extract from *Waiting for the All Clear* by B Wicks (1990); Jonathan Cape for the extracts from *Why the Allies Won* by R Overy (1995) and *Blitzkrieg* by L Deighton (1979); Century Hutchinson for the extracts from *Don't you know there's a war on?* by J Croall (1989); Collins for the extract from *The Collins Encyclopedia of Military History* by E & T Dupuy (ed) (1993); Collins and Brown for the extract from *British History* by J Gardiner & N Wenborn (ed) (1995); Coronet for the extracts from *Finest Hour* by T Clayton & P Craig (1999); Crowell for the extracts from *World War 1939-1945* by P Young (1966); The Daily Mail for the extract from *The Daily Mail* (June 1940); Granada for the extract from *Goodbye Darkness* by W Manchester (1985); Grange Books for the extract from *The Experience of World War Two* by J Campbell (ed) (1989); Grapevine/Thorsons Publishing Group for the extract from *Women at War* by S Saywell (1985); Greenhill Books for the extract from *War on the Eastern Front* by J Lucas (1991); The Guardian for the extract from *The Guardian* (October, 1938); Hamlyn for the extract from *The Military History of World War II* by B Pitt (ed) (1986); Harper Collins for the extract from *For Five Shillings a Day* by R Begg & P Liddle (ed) (2002); Heinemann for the extract from *The Forties* by A Jenkins (1977); Hyman Unwin for the extracts from *The Rise and Fall of the Great Powers* by P Kennedy (1988); Mandarin for the extract from *London at War* by P Ziegler (1996); Marshall Cavendish for the extract from *The War Years, 1939-45: Eyewitness Accounts* by J Lucas (1994); Methuen for the extract from *Infamy* by J Toland (1982); John Murray for the extract from *An Underworld at War* by D Thomas (2003); the extracts from *The Oxford Companion to the Second World War* by I C B Dear (Gen. ed) (1995), the extract from *The USA, 1917-1980* by N Smith (1996) and the extract from *Britain and Europe* by J Joll (ed) (1967) by permission of Oxford University Press; Pan for the extract from *The First Casualty* by P Knightly (1975); Penguin for the extracts from *Total War* by P Calvocoressi (1972) and *Britain in the Modern World* by E Nash & A Newth (1967); Readers Digest for the extract from *Life on the Home Front* by T Healey (1993); The Spectator for the extract from *The Spectator* (September, 1940); Thames Methuen for the extracts from *A People's War* by P Lewis (1986); Thames Television for the material from *A People's War* (1986) (a Thames Television programme); Triad Panther for the extract from *Fighter* by L Deighton (1979); William Morrow for the extract from *Barbarossa* by A Clark (1965); Viking for the extracts from *Stalingrad* by A Beevor (1998); Virago Books for the extract from *Hearts Undefeated* by J Hartley (ed) (1994).

Every effort has been made to trace and acknowledge ownership of copyright. The publishers will be glad to make suitable arrangements with any copyright holders whom it has not been possible to contact.

Note about the Internet links in the book. The user should be aware that URLs or web addresses change regularly. Every effort has been made to ensure the accuracy of the URLs provided in this book on going to press. It is inevitable, however, that some will change. It is sometimes possible to find a relocated web page, by just typing in the address of the home page for a website in the URL window of your browser.

Artwork by Art Construction.

Orders: please contact Bookpoint Ltd, 130 Milton Park, Abingdon, Oxon OX14 4SB. Telephone: (44) 01235 827720. Fax: (44) 01235 400454. Lines are open from 9.00 – 6.00, Monday to Saturday, with a 24 hour message answering service. You can also order through our website www.hoddereducation.co.uk.

British Library Cataloguing in Publication Data
A catalogue record for this title is available from the British Library

ISBN-13: 978 0 340 81421 5

First Published 2004
Impression number   11
Year   2015

Copyright © Neil DeMarco 2004

Cover image shows Give 'Em Both Barrels, poster by Jean Carlu, 1942 © Swim Inc/CORBIS.
Typeset by Fakenham Photosetting Limited Fakenham, Norfolk.
Printed in Dubai for Hodder Education, an Hachette UK Company, Carmelite House,
50 Victoria Embankment, London EC4Y 0DZ